Policing in Europe
Uniform in Diversity

Bill Tupman &
Alison Tupman

intellect™

EXETER, ENGLAND

First published in Great Britain by **Intellect Books**
School of Art and Design, Earl Richards Road North, Exeter EX2 6AS

Series Editor: Keith Cameron
Copy Editor: Lucy Kind
Cover Design: Amanda Brown
Cover Illustration: Peter Davies

A catalogue record for this book is available from the British Library

ISBN 1-871516-90-0

Printed and bound in Great Britain by Cromwell Press, Wiltshire

Contents

intellect

EUROPEAN STUDIES SERIES

General Editor   Keith Cameron

Humour and History	Keith Cameron (ed)
The Nation: Myth or Reality?	Keith Cameron (ed)
Regionalism in Europe	Peter Wagstaff (ed)
Women in European Theatre	Elizabeth Woodrough (ed)
Children and Propaganda	Judith Proud
The New Russia	Michael Pursglove (ed)
English Language in Europe	Reinhard Hartmann (ed)
Food in European Literature	John Wilkins (ed)
Theatre and Europe	Christopher McCullough
European Identity in Cinema	Wendy Everett (ed)
Television in Europe	James A. Coleman & Brigitte Rollet (eds)
Language, Community and the State	Dennis Ager
Women Voice Men	Maya Slater (ed)
National Identity	Keith Cameron (ed)
Policing in Europe	Bill Tupman & Alison Tupman
Regionalism in the European Union	Peter Wagstaff (ed)
Spaces in European Cinema	Myrto Konstantarakos (ed)

Introduction

Between 1988 and 1994, Bill Tupman visited police services in 10 of the (then) 12 European Union states, as Director of The Centre for Police and Criminal Justice Studies at the University of Exeter. Alison Tupman, initially as tutor responsible for the MA dissertations, and later as Acting Director, also visited services in 5 countries, and many constabularies in England and Wales. Greece and Luxembourg were the exceptions, but as compensation of a sort, both Bill and Alison visited and ran courses for police officers in Cyprus, an applicant for EU membership, and Bill also visited the police in Gdansk, Poland.

Wherever they could they visited police stations, control rooms, training colleges and talked informally to officers. This gives them an unusual and, for academics, perhaps a unique perspective on European policing. As outsiders, it was at first strange and confusing, but they had the advantage of accompanying groups of police officers who were their MA students. The original objectives of these visits were to gain an understanding of the implications of '1992' when internal European borders were to be abolished as a consequence of the Single European Act. The authors argued fiercely about what they found; about whether 'they' really did things so differently, or whether legal and political frameworks were as important in influencing police behaviour as criminal and crowd behaviour. In the majority of cases the problems facing police officers in Europe were pretty much the same.

The MA students, who came from 35 different countries, including Africa and the Middle East as well as the UK, quickly came to an agreement with their colleagues in Europe that the rank structures, uniforms worn, managerial doctrine, structures of judicial and political accountability and methods of financing were largely irrelevant. What was different was the relationship between police and public. What mattered was whether the public were hostile or friendly. Where they were friendly they were likely to provide assistance and less likely to be violent during demonstrations or in crowds. What the students argued about amongst themselves and with their hosts was whether this was related to the way the police behaved or to the nature of the society they were policing. So, despite the diversity of organisations and the uniforms worn, the experience was largely about identifying the uniformities under the diversity. The demands of the job appeared to remain more or less the same: patrol either on foot or in cars, arrest, paperwork, occasional involvement with other officers in crowd management, which might or might not involve violent confrontation, and assisting the public generally in emergencies. There was general disdain for police officers further up the hierarchy who were seen as having 'desk jobs' and therefore remote from the realities of front line policing. It was also interesting to see the students listening to presentations from senior police officers in which the latter demonstrated that they were very aware of the problems of the front line police officer, and that restructuring and other changes were intended to increase the ability of the front line officer to deliver the service demanded by the public.

Bill Tupman's awareness of the concerns of senior police officers is also quite comprehensive as he has been giving lectures to senior police officers since 1972. His awareness of the concerns of middle rank officers comes from the fact that after 1978 he was very much involved in the Inspectors' Development Course for South West Region, setting and marking essays for the course and thus getting quite a sharp insight into the police perspective on events. He was also lecturing on democracy and the rule of law, public order, industrial relations and a number of topics that were fairly sensitive in the years between 1979 and the end of the Miners' Strike in 1985.

It was involvement in these courses that led to the establishment of the MA in Police Studies and the Centre for Police and Criminal Justice Studies at Exeter University. Inspectors who had completed essays wanted to know, 'now, what?' The answer was to create full-time and part-time variants of the MA, the part-time option being taken by officers from over 40 of the 52 UK constabularies. Student pressure also led to the creation of the study tours, which visited Scotland, the Royal Ulster Constabulary of Northern Ireland and the Garda Síochána of Ireland as well as continental Europe. Hundreds of research dissertations were written over the decade of the Centre's existence. Under the influence of John Alderson, retired Chief Constable of Devon and Cornwall and Rear Admiral John Bell, a major European Conference on Policing Europe after 1992 was hosted by the Centre in Exeter in 1989.

The late 1980s and early 1990s were particularly interesting years to visit police services because so many changes were taking place. Some of these were physical; some were developments in policing doctrines. The authors observed the creation of new police organisations, such as the Ertzaintza in the Basque country. The Irish police college at Templemore was transformed from a grey barracks block, looming out of the mists of the British colonial tradition, into a modern light-coloured edifice fit to house the new training programmes instituted by the Walsh Report. Slowly patterns emerged. There was initially a confusion of uniforms and suits, for it was impossible to talk with police officers without talking to judges, procurators, civil servants and even politicians. For example, some of the Assistant Chief Constables the study tour met in Denmark were in reality young law graduates, tasked with prosecution. One year, the study tour visited the police college at Appeldoorn in the Netherlands and the Commandant apologised for the absence of his deputy as he was standing as a candidate in the local elections. The notion of police separation from politics is not general in Europe. Impartiality in the application of the law does not necessarily imply excluding police officers from participation in the political process, nor the exclusion of judicial authorities from participation in the investigative process. Discovering what this meant in practice, as opposed to what it meant on paper, was a fascinating voyage of exploration. It took the authors a long way from English conceptions of policing.

Between 1988 and 1994 the Schengen Agreement and Convention were transformed from a series of ideas into practical policies and frameworks for cross-border police cooperation. It was a shock to discover that many internal frontiers no longer had passport checks and that '1992' was not just pie-in-the-sky. In 1989, the Iron Curtain came down and the tour had the poignant experience of visiting the German border police, the BGS (Bundesgrenzschutz) in Lübeck just after the demolition of the Berlin Wall and the border zone between East and West Germany. For everyone there was a symbolic moment when the Commandant of the BGS took the group to the old border where they met a former East German police officer who was returning the German flag that he had borrowed for an athletics event the previous weekend. There was a strange contrast between the paramilitary uniform, based on that of the Second World War American Army, worn by the BGS officer, and the green East European non-military uniform of the East German.

The authors had one advantage over their students. Visiting the same countries on several occasions made it easier to realise that, although it was easy to get lost in the detail of practical and institutional differences, in fact there was a restricted range of historical, political, economic and social factors lying behind them. The different ways of organising policing were in fact different countries' answers to common questions such as 'to whom should the police be accountable? Who should oversee investigation? What should be the relationship between local police forces, local and national government? Do rural and urban areas require different forms of policing?'

The purpose of this book is to show that, although there is apparently a bewildering diversity of organisations involved in policing the European Union, there is greater uniformity than initially meets the eye. Currently there is a great deal of change and reform taking place and the process is not yet complete. Nevertheless, the policy makers in individual countries are facing a finite number of issues and it is possible to make general comments that will assist in understanding the changes taking place. The pressure is on for what the Germans call 'harmonization' of methods of policing in the European Union and the future is more likely to be one of greater uniformity than greater diversity.

The themes of this book, then, are uniformity and diversity. The first chapter provides an overview of the English model of policing, a framework for classifying European policing systems and some basic facts and figures in tabular form. The second chapter examines the sources of diversity and traces them back to the origins of the various organisations that became police. The third and fourth chapters provide a perspective on the uniformity behind the diversity. By taking the continental division between the policing missions of repression and prevention as their theme, they seek to demonstrate that there is diversity in the structures within which the missions are carried out; although the missions are carried out by all the organisations across the whole of the European Union. The fifth chapter addresses issues of legitimacy and accountability. The sixth chapter deals with the pressures for change and in particular the cross border framework. The final chapter discusses where the whole system is going and tries to predict what the balance between uniformity and diversity will be when the process is complete.

The authors would like to acknowledge the assistance given them by two people who have both read several drafts of this work: firstly, Professor Keith Cameron, who has had to do much more editorial work than can usually be expected of a series editor. Bill and Alison are both grateful for his patience, and his understanding that two people recovering from chronic illnesses require delicate handling. This book represents occupational therapy of an unusually difficult kind. They would also like to express their thanks to Professor Roy Wilkie for encouraging them to persist and convincing them that they had something worth saying about policing in Western Europe despite the incoherent nature of early drafts.

1. Models of Policing

Introduction
This Chapter outlines some salient features of policing in England and Wales, to highlight the striking differences between this system and other European systems. Variables such as population size, and number of police officers (sworn and civilian), are used to indicate the kinds of factors that may underlie apparent differences. European policing systems are then divided into three broad groups as a precondition for the detailed discussion to follow in later chapters.

English Policing
Most misconceptions about the British police service begin with the image that many people have from film and television. The media still love to talk of 'Scotland Yard' as if it were a centralised organisation called in when local police services fail, which is clearly not the case. It is not even generally realised that there are a number of different legal systems in the UK: those of England and Wales, Scotland, Northern Ireland and the quite separate systems operating in the Isle of Man and the Channel Islands. Some would even argue that there are at least 52 different policing systems — one for each constabulary.

New Scotland Yard is the headquarters of the Metropolitan Police which is one of the 43 constabularies of England and Wales. The 'Met' is responsible for policing the capital of the UK, London, with the exception of the City of London, the financial heart of the UK which for historical reasons has its own police force. There are other metropolitan police forces which police the largest conurbations in England and Wales: these are West Midlands Constabulary (Birmingham), the Greater Manchester Police, Merseyside Police (Liverpool), West Yorkshire (Leeds), South Yorkshire (Sheffield) and Northumbria (Newcastle). In many ways the South Wales Constabulary is also primarily a metropolitan Constabulary. All the other constabularies police areas which are a mixture of urban and rural.

The 51 police forces in England, Wales and Scotland are each headed by a Chief Constable who is accountable to a Police Authority. The English and Welsh forces come under the governmental direction of the Home Office; the Scottish Home Office deals with Scotland. Prior to the Police Act of 1964 there were over 100 constabularies, based in urban boroughs or rural counties. In the urban boroughs, accountability was to a Watch Committee which was primarily composed of elected local politicians. In the counties, accountability was to a mixture of Justices of the Peace and elected county councillors. The distinction between the policing of urban and rural areas is one that still exists in the rest of continental Europe. After 1964 the distinction between rural and urban policing was abolished as the different constabularies were amalgamated into unitary territorial authorities based on the new local government boundaries. The Chief Constable became an independent figure responsible for day-to-day policing of the force area and responsible to both the Home Office and the Police Authority. Until the reforms of John Major's Conservative government a Police Authority consisted of both representatives of the judiciary and representatives from elected local councils.

In Scotland there are 8 constabularies corresponding to the 8 former regional governments of Scotland. The closest to an urban constabulary is that of Strathclyde which includes the city of Glasgow, although Lothian and Borders Constabulary also covers Edinburgh, and Grampian Constabulary includes Aberdeen. These are huge in terms of the geographical area covered, although relatively small in terms of the number of constables employed. Dumfries and Galloway, for example, has around 400 constables and was unfortunate enough to be the constabulary in which the Lockerbie air disaster occurred — in resource terms, a logistic nightmare for that force. The system in Scotland also differs in that, as well as political accountability, there is judicial accountability to the Procurator Fiscal for the conduct of criminal investigation. Scotland shares the procuratorial system with the rest of continental northern Europe. It is especially close to the system that now exists in the Netherlands, which instituted reforms in the late 1980s.

Northern Ireland has a single police service, the Royal Ulster Constabulary, with a single Chief Constable. Because of the problem of terrorism in Northern Ireland, since 1968, policing has taken on a paramilitary role: the police are armed, their vehicles are armoured and they are relatively permanently assisted by the military. The nearest parallel in the rest of Europe would probably be the Guardia Civil in the Basque country, or the Carabinieri during the campaign of the Red Brigades in the cities of northern Italy. Other comparisons could be made with the permanent paramilitary police organisations that can be grouped together under the generic title 'gendarmerie'.

In total contrast, the Channel Islands have an almost mediaeval system of policing, similar to that which existed in most of the UK before the creation of the modern police in 1829. In addition, there are police services not covered by the Home Office including the Royal Military Police, the Ministry of Defence Police, the UK Atomic Energy Police and the British Transport Police. As well as these organisations, there are also other police organisations with specialist roles, such as political policing which is carried out in this country by the Special Branch and in Germany by the Office for the Protection of the Constitution. There are also bodies which we do not think of as being police but which do carry out specific policing roles, for example, fiscal policing is carried out in the UK by the Customs and Excise Service, which deals with the levying of duties on imports and the pursuit of duty evaders and other individuals and companies seeking to smuggle in illegal goods, or goods on which insufficient duty has been paid. Most of the UK's European neighbours also have customs services with greater or lesser amounts of power. Italy is unusual in having a Guardia di Finanza which deals with all forms of fiscal policing. The Immigration Service exists to exclude illegal immigrants from the country. It and the coastguard are perhaps the closest we come in the UK to a border police, which in Germany involves the existence of a major paramilitary organisation, the Bundesgrenzschutz. In other countries in Europe this is one of the roles taken on by the gendarmerie.

English anomalies

Moving on from internal differences between the UK forces, it may not be realised by readers from England, Scotland, Wales or Northern Ireland that to view the police as a unified organisation delivering a service over a defined territory is actually quite unusual. If one looks at the continent there is a stronger division of police roles and functions, manifesting the notion that different organisations deliver different types of service in different types of territory. Citizens of the UK before 1964 would not find this so strange, for the policing that was delivered then differed according to whether the area was rural or urban; there was also a commonly perceived difference between a uniform police and a plain clothes detective police, mainly because the urban areas were much more likely to possess a plain clothes detective force. It was the county forces and smaller urban district constabularies that had to 'send for the Yard'.

On the continent the distinction between rural and urban policing has not been reformed and the requirement for a variety of paramilitary roles has led to quite separate organisations and quite separate financing of policing in rural and urban areas. In this country uniform officers are increasingly involved in minor investigation as a normal part of their daily work, but on the continent patrol work and criminal investigation each involve offficers in accountability to different authorities and sometimes may mean an officer's temporary transfer to an organisation with a different nomenclature - the police judiciaire.

The general point is that the notion of the British copper, multi-functional, omnicompetent, is not one shared by most continental governments. Whereas in England and Wales since 1964 it has been possible to say that 'a copper is a copper is a copper', responsible simply to the law and, until 1985, carrying out prosecution him or herself, the copper on the streets of the continent is actually responsible to different organisations according to which aspect of duty is being carried out. In those different roles the officer has different organisational channels of responsibility and accountability.

Another difference between England and Wales and many of its continental neighbours lies in the English conception of the police as civilian rather than military. This belief underpinned the establishment of the New Police in 1829 by Sir Robert Peel in response to the massacre at Peterloo in Manchester. This is not a road travelled by the majority of other European countries. It was forced on the Germans in 1945 by the Americans; the Dutch also decided to adopt similar measures as a result of their failures to deal with rioting in the streets in the 1970s. The Greeks also civilianised in 1984. But, on the whole, the notion of the police being civilians in uniform is not one that has been univerally accepted by governments on the continent. The police may have had to become civilians in uniform in many cities, but the distrust governments feel for city populations has led many to maintain a semi-military force as a reserve in the rural areas. Such forces have also had a secondary role in wartime, policing the battlefield to prevent desertion.

Not only the police of England and Wales, but also those of Scotland, Northern Ireland and Ireland, differ from continental police in not having a separately recruited officer class. With the exception of the Garda Síochána in Ireland, there are graduate entry schemes which make provision for graduates to enter a 'fast track' to promotion, yet they still must join as constables. Governments on the continent are much happier to have an officer class recruited from a different social and educational background to that of the constabulary in general. However, when one actually examines the continental organisations it turns out that 50 per cent of the officer corps is promoted from within the ranks and 50 per cent is direct entrant.

This brief examination of differences in the police systems in the UK raises many of the issues that will be looked at in greater depth later in the book:

- different ways of arranging responsibility according to the role being performed;
- the impact of judicial, rather than police, responsibility for overseeing investigation;
- the degree to which there is a form of judicial accountability;
- the involvement of different levels of government in the system of accountability;
- the degree to which a police service is under national or local control;
- the ways in which specialised roles are organised and controlled;
- the degree to which the police are civilian or military;
- the degree to which the police are undergoing a process of reform.

Police and Public

Tables I and II show two slightly different ways of answering the question, 'how intensively policed are the states of the European Union?', depending on whether one only includes sworn officers in calculating the ratio of police to population, or also includes civilian employees of the police. Some countries are considerably further along the road of civilianisation than others. The UK, for example, has greatly extended the roles in which civilians are employed since Home Office Circular 114/83 and one now finds civilians not only as Scene of Crime Officers (SOCOs) but also in licensing checks for firearms and explosives. These are the kinds of roles which bring them into contact with the public.

The countries in Table I have been arranged according to the ratio of sworn officers to population: the larger the ratio, the greater the number of citizens per officer. Where there is no sworn officer figure given for a country, the country did not return a separate figure to the United Nations and the ratio for that country is the same in both Table I and II. This could either be because all tasks are performed by sworn officers, or because an incorrect return has been made due to misunderstandings about the information required.

Table I needs to be treated with caution. It does not indicate how intensively a populace was policed, because it does not record how officers are deployed. There are some quite large discrepancies that suggest very real differences exist between the countries. Although Northern Ireland's ratio may be explained in terms of the terrorist troubles, the difference between England and Wales on the one hand and Ireland, on the other, or between Belgium and the Netherlands, are significant and require explanation.

	Pop (mill)	Total police	Total sworn Police	Officer: n. population ratio
Northern Ireland	1.5	11,691	8,489	1:177
France	55.3	260,800		1:212
Greece	9.8	39,335	37,910	1:259
Portugal	10.1	37,735		1:268
Belgium	9.9	36,613		1:270
Ireland	3.5		12,200	1:287
Italy	56.7	200,660	192,817	1:294
Spain	38.5	119,315	111,129	1:346
Austria	7.6	27,705	21,715	1:350
West Germany	61.1	197,230	168,312	1:363
Scotland	5.1	17,783	13,841	1:368
Netherlands	14.6	37,988		1:384
Eng and Wales	50.9	172,495	127,090	1:401
Luxembourg	0.36	811		1:444
Denmark	5.1	13,292	10,272	1:496
Sweden	8.34	22,558	16,351	1:510
Finland	5.0	11,942	8,467	1:591

Table I. The ratio of sworn officers to population in EU member States, 1990[1]

The picture demonstrated conforms quite well to English prejudices. England and Wales and the Scandinavian countries appear to be quite lightly policed. France is clearly very heavily policed; almost as heavily policed in fact as Northern Ireland. The similarity of policing levels between West Germany and Scotland could be surprising to the average Briton, as it might have been expected that West Germany was another highly policed society, but this appears to be based on pre-war prejudice rather than experience.

Table II demonstrates what happens when civilian employees are included. By including the total police, a country's population is divided by a larger figure and so it looks as though the populace is more intensively policed. According to the data

	Pop (mill)	Total police	Total sworn Police	Total civilian personnel	Officer: n. population ratio
Northern Ireland	1.5	11,691[2]	8,489		1:128
France	55.3	260,800			1:212
Greece	9.8	39,335	37,910	1,425	1:249
Portugal	10.1	37,735		0	1:268
Belgium	9.9	36,613			1:270
Austria	7.6	27,705	21,715	5,990	1:274
Italy	56.7	200,660	192,817	7,843	1:283
Ireland	3.5		12,200		1:287
Scotland	5.1	17,783	13,841	3,942	1:287
Eng and Wales	50.9	172,495	127,090	45,405	1:295
West Germany	61.1	197,230	168,312	28,918	1:310
Spain	38.5	119,315	111,129	8,186	1:323
Sweden	8.34	22,558	16,351	6,207	1:370
Denmark	5.1	13,292	10,272	3,020	1:384
Netherlands	14.6	37,988		0	1:384
Finland	5.0	11,942	8,467	3,475	1:419
Luxembourg	0.36	811			1:444

Table II The ratio of all police to population in EU member States, 1990

returned to the UN, Portugal and the Netherlands do not employ any civilians at all; nor do France, Belgium, Luxembourg and Ireland. It is unclear whether the difference between the total police and total sworn officers for Northern Ireland is made up by the full-time reserve or whether there are also civilian employees.

Countries differed widely in their attitude towards employing civilians in 1990: some, especially those with a paramilitary role, only employed sworn officers, no matter what the task, because of a requirement that all employees be subject to military discipline; others used civilians only for clerical work, while others employed them in a variety of roles.

France remains the most heavily policed country with Greece close behind. The Scandinavian countries and anomalous Luxembourg continue to appear the most lightly policed countries in Europe. England and Wales now join a broad band of countries with surprisingly similar ratios of police to population. As other European countries follow the British model and civilianise, the picture presented by both Tables I and II will converge and the uniformity hiding behind the apparent diversity will assert itself.

	Total police	Total sworn Police	Total civilian personnel	Civilian percentage in police
Greece	39,335	37,910	1,425	3.62%
Italy	200,660	192,817	7,843	3.91%
Spain	119,315	111,129	8,186	6.86%
West Germany	197,230	168,312	28,918	14.66%
Austria	27,705	21,715	5,990	21.62%
Scotland	17,783	13,841	3,942	22.17%
Denmark	13,292	10,272	3,020	22.72%
Eng and Wales	172,495	127,090	45,405	26.32%
Sweden	22,558	16,351	6,207	27.52%
Finland	11,942	8,467	3,475	29.10%

Table III. Civilian employees as a percentage of total police 1990

Table III calculates the percentage of a country's total police that is civilian, using the same data as Table II, in which only ten countries returned figures for civilian employees.

This calculation shows that there are very great differences in the proportion of civilian employees, reflecting different attitudes towards what may be done by a civilian and what must be done by a sworn police officer. The countries with civilian proportions of over 20 per cent are those whose ratios moved upwards in Table II, giving a smaller number of members of the population per member of the police. But whether this amounts to more intensive policing depends on just how these members of the police are deployed. If it is on paperwork, then perhaps there is little difference in the number of officers on the street.

If one were to argue that employment of civilians implies greater efficiency in dealing with administrative tasks, it could be argued that perhaps some countries' procedures are more bureaucratic and require more such staff. One argument in this country for the employment of civilians was that it would enable the release of officers to do 'real' police work and would improve operational efficiency. The jury is still out on whether this in fact has been the result.

It is worth noting at this point that the figures for the UK do not include the Special Constabulary. This is an organisation of part-time volunteers whose importance has fluctuated over recent years. Funding shortages have recently tended to enhance the role played by the Specials and they should really be included in the Tables, but one would have to decide the proportion of a full-time sworn officer represented by a part-time volunteer Special. The UN does not have returns for part-time and auxiliary officers, which may conceal another discrepancy.

There are other reasons why the number of officers varies. One possibility is that it reflects the government's expectation that it will have to deal with violence or public disorder. Such events might be terrorist or paramilitary in nature, rioting or industrial relations-related demonstrations, picketing or civil protest and the like. Or perhaps it reflects differences in the social history of the countries. At first sight this seems unlikely, for although Northern Ireland was and is the only country currently dealing with almost daily terrorist activity, terrorism has been by no means absent from Spain. France has a healthy tradition of agricultural protest and Italy one of organised crime; Greece, Italy and West Germany were dealing with immigration problems and Ireland, the overspill from the troubles in Northern Ireland as well as rural depopulation. The variation in ratios might reflect differences in the size of the territory, but, looking at the bottom of Table I, it can be seen that the wide tracts of Finland and the compact area of Luxembourg receive similarly low levels of policing. Whichever factor is considered, from the state of the economy to the degree of urbanisation, there is a country with a similar ratio in which that factor does not appear to play a part.

Perhaps the way in which a country's police is organised affects numbers. The next Table categorises countries according to types of policing system. The type of system in a country is not random: it results from historic and geographic factors; in the case of Table V, especially those associated with war, invasion and conquest.

Making sense of European policing: a framework

Table IV divides the countries of Europe into three categories: 'Napoleonic', 'National' and 'Decentralised'. There is movement taking place between categories which blurs the picture slightly. Germany became decentralised on the US model in 1945, Greece changed after the fall of the colonels, and Spain is in a process of change which is not yet complete and the outcome of which is unclear. A brief explanation of each category follows, accompanied by a Table of relevant statistical material for each category. There is variation within categories and there are other variables that can be used to classify European countries and their policing structures on a different basis.

The Napoleonic system is, as the name suggests, an inheritance from the days of the Napoleonic Empire. In these eight countries that system has stayed largely unchanged since the 19th century[3], being based on a division of policing into two types, with an accompanying division of organisational structure and responsibility right up to government level. A paramilitary organisation responsible to the Ministry of Defence polices the countryside (the Gendarmerie)and a civilian organisation responsible to the Ministry of the Interior polices the cities (Home Office Police). The Police Judiciaire are the investigative arm of the police, used for all activities concerned with crime rather than regular patrolling. In addition, the 'Other' police, such as Italy's Guardia di Finanza or the Marechausee in the Netherlands, are special organisations of police to deal with specific crime priorities or tasks; their existence simply reflects the tasks that government considers important.

Napoleonic	National	Decentralised
Austria		
Belgium		
	Denmark	
	Finland since 1997	Finland before 1997
France		
Greece until 1984	Greece post-1984	
		Germany
	Ireland	
Italy		
Luxembourg		
Netherlands until 1990		Netherlands after 1990
Portugal		
Spain		Spain
	Sweden after 1965	Sweden before 1965
		UK

Table IV A framework for classifying European policing systems

	Pop (mill)	Home Office police	Gend-armerie	P.J.[a]	Other	Total police 1990	Ratio as Table I
Italy	56.7	80,000	85,000	14,000	92,000[b]	200,660	1:283
France	55.3	163,000	92,000	5,800		260,800	1:212
Portugal	10.1	17,600	18,800	1,565	8,200	37,735	1:268
Belgium	9.9	18,248	16,970	1,395		36,613	1:270
Spain	38.5	53,000	72,000	all	N/K[c]	119,315	1:323
Netherlands[d]	14.6	25,000	14,500	none	4,500[e]	37,988	1:384
Luxembourg	0.36	414	397			811	1:484
Austria	7.6	n/a	n/a	none		27,705	1:274

Table V. Napoleonic Model[4]

a   Police Judiciaire
b   The Guardia di Finanza and the Polizia Urbana
c   Police of the Autonomous Communities

d   Netherlands' system before the reforms of the late 1980s
e   The Marechausee

	Pop (mill)	Total police 1990	ratio as Table I
Greece	9.8	39,335	1:249
Ireland	3.5	12,200	1:287
Sweden	8.34	22,558	1:370
Denmark	5.1	13,292	1:384
Finland	5.0	11,942	1:419

Table VI. National model

It is worth noting that, although these police services all share a common tradition in one sense, the ratio of officers to population varies just as wildly as if they did not.

In the National category the Scandinavian countries of Denmark, Finland and Sweden are grouped together with Ireland and Greece. Greece was a Napoleonic system until 1984. Sweden was a decentralised system before 1965 and Finland has also recently moved from decentralised to national. These are ethnically homogenous countries with relatively low populations. In a 'national police service' all members of a force, whether civilian or sworn police officers, may work anywhere in the country's territory and are ultimately subject to a single police chief, responsible to a unified single national political authority, rather than to a more local political authority. The policing task is unified, in that there is no separate organisational provision for different types of police.

As with the Napoleonic grouping, the ratios relate better to whether or not the country is in the Scandinavian group than to it being a national force.

The decentralised model essentially refers to the relative autonomy of police recruitment, decision-making and accountability in police force areas that are subdivisions of the geographic area of the country. Yet there is a wide variation beyond this similarity. The UK and Germany have quite different, decentralised, policing structures. West Germany followed an updated variant of the American model which was effectively imposed on it after the end of the Second World War in 1945. Although the majority of the West German police are divided into territorially separate Länder authorities, there are also numerically significant national police services, such as the Bundeskriminalamt (BKA) which is equivalent to the American FBI, and the Bundesgrenzschutz. In total there are 12 national police services in Germany, the other most significant service being the BfV, the Office for the Protection of the Constitution.

The German system merits discussion, because the Germans are the source of pressure on the other countries of the EU for harmonisation of policing to meet the threats associated with cross border crime. It has been said that Germany already views the Netherlands and Belgium as equivalent to another Land and that they would like to see similar regional systems adopted elsewhere; arguably in the UK we already have such a system in embryo in the regional organisation of crime squads and of Her Majesty's Inspectorate of Constabulary.

The German/US model of decentralisation may be in competition with the Anglo/Dutch form, so to place all three countries with Spain, in the decentralised model, is an oversimplification. It would be better to talk of the 'county' decentralised model and the 'province' decentralised model. England and Wales, with the Netherlands, have a county model of decentralisation, whereas Northern Ireland and the Spanish areas of Catalonia and the Basque country have a province model. Scotland does not fit neatly

	Pop (mill)	Number of units	Total police 1990	ratio as Table I
Germany (all)		16		
Northern Ireland	1.5	1	8,489	1:128
Scotland	5.1	8	17,783	1:287
England	50.9	43	172,495	1:295
West Germany	61.1	10	197,230	1:310
Netherlands[a]	14.6	25	37,988	1:384

Table VII. Decentralised model

a   Netherlands' system after the reforms of the late 1980s

into either and falls somewhere between the two, as police service boundaries and local government boundaries no longer coincide.

It might have been more equitable to put Northern Ireland into the category of a province policed like a German Land. The Basque Country and Catalonia could then have been added to the same category. The complexity of Western European policing systems is that some countries have areas which are policed in a way quite contrary to the norm followed by the rest of the country.

The Dutch reform of the late 1980s was intended to follow what the Dutch authorities called the 'county' model of England and Wales. By this they meant a unified policing structure that covered territorial areas of the country regardless of whether they were rural or urban. The Netherlands was divided into 25 such areas. Each police service was a unitary authority: one police force under the control of a chief constable was responsible for delivering services to the inhabitants of the territorial area. A 26th constabulary included the criminal intelligence agency and various support functions that were seen as appropriately provided at the national level. Since this reform the UK has followed in creating NCIS, the National Criminal Intelligence Service and the National Crime Squad. Scotland's system is a hybrid between the systems of the Netherlands and England and Wales: although it also is divided into local autonomous units, it follows the Dutch in having a Procurator for a law officer who is responsible for the supervision of investigation of crime. When examined in these terms, Northern Ireland's system is quite separate and can be seen as a national system for a sub-unit of a nation; using this criterion it could be placed in Table VI.

Quite why West Germany, with the largest population, should only have had 10 territorial units when the UK has 52, has a great deal to do with pressure from America for a federal system at the end of the Second World War and the units that emerged from the zones of occupation after 1945. The number of units in the UK relates more to the history of local government structure and the specificity of regional identifications than to anything else. The nature of the national voting system, voting patterns, deliberate political manipulations such as changes in electoral boundaries, and economic and social factors such as industrialisation are also factors that may be expected to affect the internal organisation of decentralised systems. In this category, as with the others, there is no similarity in the police: population ratio.

Conclusion

While there are clearly some quite complex difficulties involved in comparing the police forces of the European Union, equally there are some recurrent themes. There is a variety of ways in which a country's policing may be organised yet there is considerable agreement on those tasks and functions which it is thought necessary for the police to do. Once one enters the realms of asking to whom, and for what, the police should be accountable or which type of police officer is suitable for what, variation enters the picture.

Without quite realising it, the citizens of each country may have quite different assumptions about the treatment they expect to receive from the police. It may be a shock for an English person to realise that some of the officers patrolling the streets of Paris are in fact conscripts on National Service; to see armed police routinely in Italy; or to be stopped and fined immediately in Spain for traffic offences such as speeding.

The next chapter goes into this vexed question of who a police officer is, and what it is he or she is expected to do, by examining where the various policing roles came from historically. It also discusses how these roles have translated into the organisation of policing and the different ways in which concern for legitimacy and accountability have affected that organisation.

1   This table is based on returns made to the United Nations statistical section held at the University of Vienna. Returns were not made for Belgium, France, Ireland, Luxembourg and Northern Ireland. Entries under these categories have been taken from different sources by the authors or calculated where necessary. The Netherlands and Portugal did not make a return for civilian employees and a figure of zero was assumed to be the case. The final column was calculated by dividing Column 2 by Column 4, or by Column 3 where no figure was returned for Sworn Police.
2   Including full time reserve
3   This was true only up until the late 1980s for the Netherlands, when large scale reforms took place.
4   The figures in this table are not those from the UN but have been extracted from A F Semerak et al *Die Polizeien in Westeuropa*, Stuttgart, Boorberg, 1989. This gives figures for individual police organisations in particular countries where these could be obtained. No figures were provided for Austria. For Belgium, France and Luxembourg this produces the same figure as total sworn police 1990; for Portugal, Italy, Spain and the Netherlands it produces a larger figure.

2. What Is Policing?

Introduction

In the Introduction to this book it was argued that, although there may be great diversity in the organisation of policing in the EU, there is increasing uniformity in the range of roles performed by its myriad police services. While Chapters 6 and 7 will examine the pressures that are leading towards uniformity, this chapter examines the origins of existing institutions. It addresses these questions: what do we mean by 'policing'? What are the elements of the policing role, and where did they come from? Why are legitimacy and accountability such enduring issues in policing? What are the sources of the diversity in the policing structures in the EU?

What do we mean by 'policing'?

One answer to this question is that 'policing' is what the 'police' do. The problem with this is that organisations and individuals bearing the name 'police' appear to do quite different things in different parts of Europe. Uniforms differ and are sometimes indistinguishable from military uniforms. Weaponry differs: it ranges from the faithful British truncheon, which is now being replaced by the American two handled baton and even the canister of Mace, through the pistol or the semi-automatic weapon, to the armoured car with bulldozer blade and water-cannon attached. Individual officers have different powers to restrict the liberty of citizens and different degrees of discretion with regard to how and when these powers can be exercised. The colours of cars used by police organisations differ even within the same country as does the emergency telephone number for contacting the police, despite attempts at standardisation.

One of the factors behind the Single European Act and the Treaty of Maastricht is the idea that all citizens of the European Union (Maastricht, 1992) have the right to live and work anywhere in the EU, and justice demands that all are treated identically, especially by the police, or, under the European Convention of Human Rights, evidence of criminal activity will be declared inadmissible by a court and citizens will be free to sue for wrongful detention. Differences between countries in their definition of what policing is, and what the police do, will have increasing legal significance. Consequently it is of more than academic significance that participants in the criminal justice system, as well as different disciplines, stress very different aspects of the role. Members of the general public also have very different ideas of what police officers are for. The following definitions were provided during 10 years of discussion with students on the MA in Police Studies. A series of surveys in cities around the world has revealed that the public thinks the police should prioritise preventing dogs fouling the pavement and silencing noisy neighbours. There is also a persistent belief that the

Interested Party	Definition
the legal profession	a police officer is a citizen with special powers that can legally be used to deprive other citizens of their liberties; policing consists of enforcing laws
accountancy	policing is a service industry involving relationships between customers and service providers; to ensure that public money is not wasted, goals must be set for personnel, managers and equipment; achievement of goals, within budget, must be monitored. Which services are sold by the police to their customers depends totally on their price competitiveness, or in other words, what the taxpayer is prepared to pay for
The police	' I want to remain in charge of a 24 hour emergency service.' (member of the Association of Chief Police Officers (ACPO) on a senior officers' course responding to the demand that he define his core business)
criminology	a police officer is a street manager; policing is part of the system of defining crime and criminals by deciding, via the exercise of discretion, which laws to enforce and which to ignore
economic history	policing is the mechanism which, throughout history, has maintained the price structure of economic activities, including labour
economics	policing is the activity of regulating the market such that the customer has confidence in the quality, quantity and price of the goods and services being offered (derived from Hayek: this is totally opposed to the 'caveat emptor' approach of pre-Thatcher English law)
philosophy	policing is the process by which moral 'bads' are defined and the consequences for indulging in them made clear to citizens of the polity
political science	a police officer is a conflict manager, a mediator of disputes between individuals and low-level non-state actors and institutions; policing is preserving the status quo; policing is the mechanism by which the state exercises its monopoly of legitimate force in the domestic arena (the army plays the same role externally)
psychology	policing is the process of managing crowd behaviour
public administration	policing is a service provided by local government
sociology	policing is part of the system of social control
social history	policing is part of the process by which changing definitions of acceptable behaviour are arrived at/evolve
the public	according to age and/or ethnic origin the police are perceived as people to whom you report crime and bad behaviour or as hostile and prejudiced, existing to harass you

police should mediate social disputes, on occasion by dispensing summary justice on the spot, as perhaps they once did. Different sectors of the public will have different ideas about what policing is and should be.

The common core in all these different perspectives lies in the enforcement of both formal laws and rules of good behaviour at minimum cost, both of an economic kind and of 'face'. The 24-hour emergency service that police managers see themselves as providing is rarely mentioned by members of the public, as they would prefer to believe they will never require it. The right of the police to perform this enforcement, and whether they do in fact perform it equally and without favour, appears to depend on the perspective taken, suggesting that the legitimacy of what the police do is something that requires attention by institutions of the state and negotiation with those policed.

The Origins of Policing Roles

In order to understand how other countries view the police, it is necessary to construct a picture of the origins and development of police and policing. From this may be formed an understanding of the different ways the terms are used today. The police services of the individual states in Europe have different historic origins yet the tasks that they now perform come from the same, fairly limited, set of roles.

The first police officer was a religious figure, perhaps a priest, who defined correct moral behaviour, declared who had broken the code and the punishment to follow. Such people saw themselves as 'guardians of the truth'. Early societies had a low level of social differentiation; the same person would combine the roles of priest, judge, police officer and executioner. Later, as communities grew in size, there would be greater differentiation and religious sites would have temple guards.

Historical Tradition	Modern equivalent
1. Guardians of the Truth	Ideological/Religious
2. Watchmen	Private Security
3. Palace Guards	Political Police
4. Economic and other specialised organisations	Customs, Fraud Squads
5. Colonial	Assistance/Aid
6. Peoples'	New police and Proactive or Community Policing
7. Highways and Waterways	Traffic
8. Gendarmeries	Police Support Units and Reactive Policing
9. Detectives	

Table VIII. Policing roles

Some aspect of this remains in the traditional Code Napoleon concept of 'ordre public' which has a connotation of preserving public health. It also can be discerned in a general police dislike of deviation from what are seen as important social mores and norms of behaviour, whether those deviating be gypsies, immigrants, rock musicians, motorcyclists or gays. The collapse of moral consensus in European society has made it more difficult for the police to be certain what deviance is. There have been programmes to recruit into the police from these groups, to make it representative of society as it actually is at the end of the 20th century.

If it is accepted that preserving public morality was the first form of policing, it should be noted that rule-breaking and offending against the community formed an early part of the definition of what the police were empowered to watch for. Crowd management as such was a later development, as early communities would not have constituted crowds in any real sense.

Apart from obvious parallels with the Islamic police that have been set up in modern Iran and Afghanistan, there is also some continuity between the original religious police and the secular, ideological 'militias' that were set up in the Communist world after 1917. There are also institutional parallels with the reforms of Napoleon and the role of the Committees of Public Safety during the French Revolution. In the Soviet Union, the militias became more of a uniformed patrol force after the expansion of the KGB (Committee of State Security) as successor to the Cheka, OGPU and NKVD. These 'secret police' created a real threat to liberty and the right to private life, and acted as the enforcers of ideology. There is a strand of vigilantism that also connects these post-revolutionary police to their forebears in the temples of the past.

The lack of any tradition of serving a community or populace presents a major problem today for the ex-Communist police organisations of the Commonwealth of Independent States (CIS). The processes of *glasnost* and *perestroika* and economic liberalisation have produced a need for a western-style police service which can work with other police services of Europe. They lack, however, experience in the traditions of negotiating legitimacy with the public, rather than imposing it by force, and have to counter insufficient respect for their office and a great deal of mistrust and suspicion (Tupman, 1992a).

The second policing tradition named in Table VIII appeared with the development of walled cities and the appointment of the watchman, whose job it was to prevent entry to the city during the hours of darkness when citizens were not alert to thieves. Watchmen would eventually form crime prevention patrols. This element of policing continues to this day in the form of private security, which has maintained a hold in this area, particularly in the protection of industrial and commercial premises outside working hours. The watchman would also exclude from the city strangers who could not convince him of their bona-fides. This is another function that has passed to today's 'castles', the high-rise office towers and exclusive apartment blocks.

The third tradition is associated with government by an hereditary ruler. The palace guard were pledged to the physical survival of their boss, to whom they were often related. They developed a surveillance role, judging the political climate and seeking to nip conspiracies in the bud. On admittedly rare occasions, they even overthrew unpopular monarchs. This may well have been for personal gain, although it could be interpreted as a means of preventing disorder. The more modern surveillance model of the Absolute Monarchies and the security services, intelligence organisations, counter-subversion organisations and 'the office for the preservation of the constitution' (BfV in Germany), shows a clear development from the early palace guard tradition. The notion that the police should be a public service rather than a private one is partly a reaction against this tradition.

The next category results from the reality that trade and commerce were early developments in societies. Once there is a market, there will be a demand for standard weights and qualities, leading sooner rather than later to the introduction of Weights and Measures Inspectors. Similarly, it would have been recognised that there was a need to preserve the income of the State, leading to the introduction of people charged with overseeing this: tax and customs officials. They were followed by the creation of various specialist groups relating to communications, including the Royal Mail. Some of these would have been private sector rather than public organisations. In Italy the Guardia di Finanza is an unusually large organisation that fits into this category. Russia may need to develop something similar, given the government's problems in raising revenue.

There are other 'odd' police forces, whose existence appears to be related to the perception of special risk, or of areas that otherwise would not be sufficiently policed. In this country examples of these are the UK Atomic Energy Police, Ministry of Defence Police, Port Police and Parks Police.

The fifth tradition appeared with the growth of Empires, which by definition include colonies. These need some kind of force which will represent and enforce the law of the empire in situ. Documented examples usually begin with the colonial police force of the Caliphate, but there must have been Roman, Greek and Carthaginian forerunners of this. Reviews of the colonial tradition in policing history often begin by taking Peel's creation of the Royal Irish Constabulary. Perhaps bizarrely, links can be shown between the initial form of the RIC and the Caliphate, via the Moguls and their successor states in India. Students from Pakistan studying for the MA in Police Studies claimed that the Indian Army officers employed by Peel in Ireland would have obtained their ideas about policing from the system they knew in India.

The essence of British colonial policing is the combination of native traditions with a supervisory officer corps from the colonising country. The stress is on order and surveillance rather than crime control. Often the police constables were recruited from a minority tribe with religious or other differences from the majority. Where the setting up of a colonial police force has been deemed particularly successful, that country may well find its officers in demand elsewhere. As a result lineages of forms of policing can be identified: from 1922 - 1948 the Palestine police replaced the RIC as a training ground for officers, some of whom are still in advisory roles in the Arab Gulf. France, Belgium, Netherlands, Spain and Portugal would all have had colonial forces at one time or another. Ireland and Greece both have 19th century experience of being subject to colonial policing.

A discussion of the sixth category must begin from the fact that 'police' has the same origin as 'politics', i.e. *polis* or Greek city-state. In the forms of policing discussed so far it is the interests of rulers, or of religious and economic institutions, that have been buttressed by police activity. What of the interests of the people? Where the Greek city-states were democratic, almost by definition they must have pioneered the idea of a people's police, although this may have been on a tribal, or extended family, basis. Equally, there must have been similar institutions in the Roman Republic, although the *lictores* with their badge of office, the *fasces*, from which Mussolini coined the word fascism, are not a good model to take. The literature is much happier to identify the start of this tradition with the English parish constable, a role emerging from the Anglo-Saxon organisation of land and administration into Hundreds (Critchley, 1967). This may be incorrect, as there may be earlier examples from the Classical period. There should be a German parallel, given that there is a shared Anglo-Saxon past. Indeed, the common current division of police into a local and a national force in the countries of mainland Europe, suggests that the parish constable was not as unique as anglocentric literature assumes.

The essence of this form of policing is that it is not based on a 'state' organisation, but is responsible to, and part of, relatively small local communities. The Belgian 'municipality' appears to incorporate essentially the same concept, since all Belgium is divided into municipalities, paralleling English parishes. According to research undertaken by Dr J.H. Porter (1989), in the 18th century the parish constable dealt with four types of crime: vagrancy, tippling, smuggling and wrecking. Whilst the role of parish constable has now disappeared in mainland England, this system still survives in the Channel Islands.

City police forces, responsible to the city Fathers, rather than to the central government or the local aristocracy, and usually tasked with a patrol function to prevent crime, really grew out of the Watch (Reith, 1956). From these organisations emerged the 'New Police' of London, although Glasgow, Dublin, Bombay, Madras and Calcutta had created such organisations prior to Peel, Rowan and Mayne. Hangchow in China is claimed to have had such a force at the beginning of the 11th century. A full discussion of the different perspectives on what was 'new' about them can be found in Reiner (1985). They are included here as successors to the 'people's' tradition, because they are funded and raised by an urban community rather than the state .

In Italy, France and Spain, they were under-powered relative to national, surveillance-orientated, paramilitary organisations. In Belgium and the Netherlands there was a clearer delimitation of jurisdictions, although competition between Muncipal Police and Gendarmerie for the right to investigate crime was a factor in Belgium until the reforms of the early 1990s. It could be argued that 'new policing' of a slightly different variety was actually developed under Napoleon, along with the institution of the Prefect, and the Code Napoleon. Certainly in the early days there was borrowing both ways between France and England: the organisation of detectives was borrowed from Vidocq (see Chapter 3); whereas the locally-based area organisation of the Metropolitan Police was adopted in Paris.

The seventh category relates to transportation. As goods began to move between communities on a regular basis by road, water and finally, rail, organisations were created to deal with theft by highwaymen and their equivalent. In this country British Transport Police still deals with the railways, Germany still has a national Waterways Police and there are probably other varieties in existence in other countries.

The advent of the motor car led to the creation of a novel role for the police, namely the need to enforce regulations about the conduct of citizens in cars. This covers illegal parking, breaking of speed restrictions, dealing with the consequences of traffic accidents and various other functions which, some commentators have claimed, have brought the police away from the role of standing between the middle classes and the dangerous classes to a situation in which they confront the middle classes.

The similar development of the movement of information around the Internet is likely to produce a new form of policing with all the consequent conflicts that will result from enforcing rules on sectors of society who are not used to having to obey rules.

Gendarmeries, the eighth category, emerged from the need for a force to prevent desertion in battle and a corresponding need for a peace-time role for them. Right wing politicians tend to favour gendarmeries because they are accustomed to obey orders. They do not have a good track record in criminal investigation, nor are they often successful at placing the rule of law above the instructions of political figures. A military background and organisation may be useful in crowd management, where discipline and hierarchy have to take over once disorder has broken out. It is not, however, helpful in administering the criminal law, where principle has to inform discretion if a positive relationship with the public is to be maintained. Gendarmeries can score highly in public perception in terms of efficiency, whereas civilian police may be perceived to be out of their depth in times of terrorism or violent organised crime, but they can be inflexible and conservative in times when social mores are undergoing change. This book treats the Italian Carabinieri and the Spanish Guardia Civil as essentially gendarmeries.

There have sometimes been counterproductive attempts by the gendarmerie to compete for business with civilian city police, especially in Belgium before the recent reforms. In the early 1990s there was an attempt by the Belgian Home Office to merge the Gendarmerie and Municipal police, following the lines of the Dutch reform. The government unfortunately fell before the reform could be completed, but the civilianisation of the gendarmerie was successfully achieved, and lines of demarcation put in place between the two organisations with regard to criminal investigation. The recent paedophile scandal will lead to a wholesale reform of the Belgian criminal justice system, but this will still require political will to turn it into legislation

The ninth and final category is the detective: one of the last branches of policing to be created, despite the popularity of historical 'who-dun-its'. A specialist, skilled corps of men dedicated to the investigation of crime is quite a recent innovation. Although the Bow Street Runners were effectively in existence from around 1754, they were few in number and primarily interested in financial return. The Brigade de Surêté formed by Vidocq in Paris in 1810 were similarly motivated and similarly semi-official. The

Criminal Investigation department of the Metropolitan Police, surprisingly, was not created until as late as 1878 and followed the earlier Paris model (Moylan, 1934).

Relating these different traditions of policing to Table IV, the Napoleonic group combine the idea of moral guardians (*ordre public*) with palace guards and surveillance police into the gendarmerie, necessary for conscript armies. Urban communities are allowed to have a people's police of sorts, but with the gendarmerie in reserve to deal with outbreaks of socialism or other political unrest feared by the bourgeoisie. The decentralised group have chosen to concentrate on the people's police tradition, but with some specialist police at national level, increasingly including at least a criminal intelligence organisation. The national group are primarily Scandinavian, and represent a break with European historical tradition. Ireland stands alone as post-colonial in Europe, although Greece experienced Turkish colonialism in the last century.

Sources of Variation

Commentators have attempted to divide Europe on religious lines into Protestant areas and Catholic areas. This variable is supposed to govern attitudes to democracy and thus to policing. As the European Union grows, Orthodox Christian and Muslim areas may also emerge, and the religious variable may be used to explain differences in institutions and in the ways people behave. It has even been humourously suggested that the predominant type of alcohol consumed is a better variable and that spirit-drinking cultures are very different from beer-drinking cultures which, in turn, differ from wine-drinking cultures. Football hooliganism, for example, has been said to go hand-in-hand with beer-drinking rather than wine-drinking and this obviously has implications for policing. The form of trade union adopted; socialist, communist, or anarchist, can be related to a different history of protest, tactics and the likelihood of violence occurring in a conflict with employers. Thus it is impossible to discuss the differences in European policing without considering the political and cultural traditions. A major variable, relating to the traditions of policing discussed in the previous section, is that of the monarchical tradition. Where the monarchy has a constitutional tradition (e.g. England), it will also have tended towards the tradition of people's policing. Where the monarchy has clung to absolutism (e.g. France), it will tend to have a tradition of surveillance policing. Political tradition is thus an important variable, but many variables interact to product the particular policing system of a particular state or even region of a state.

One of the defining aspects of totalitarianism is that there is no mode of behaviour for a citizen that can guarantee safety from arrest, torture and imprisonment. Even joining the Party can lead to disaster. Pastor Niemoller's famous words say it all:

first they came for the communists;
and I was not a communist,
so I did not protest.

then they came for the Jews;
and I was not a Jew,
so I did not protest.

and now they are coming for me;
and there is no-one left to protest.

Such experience ensured widespread post-war support for keeping the police weak and for fragmentation of organisation. It was only possible for the Dutch to repeat the British reform of 1964 in 1990. The Belgian attempt to do likewise stalled halfway in the following year. The paedophile scandal of 1997-98 may well revive the attempt to centralise and unify Belgian policing in the near future. The Germans had, of course, already been reformed immediately post-1945. They were given the model the Americans wished they had themselves: the FBI and state police, but without the local police structures that gave the USA 40,000 different police organisations at the last count.

All the countries of the European Union except Sweden, the UK and Ireland, were affected by Fascism and the Nazi occupation. Spain and Portugal were not occupied by the Germans and kept out of the Second World War (although the Spanish Civil War can be seen as a rehearsal for it), but share in having experienced dictatorship, one party government and an excess of police power. Greece, Portugal and Spain indeed had experience of non-democratic government more recently than 1945; Portugal finally became a democracy in 1976, although this followed a brief brush with potential left-wing totalitarianism, and Spain in the post-Franco era became democratic at about the same time. The Greek military Junta fell in 1974 because of its involvement in the failed coup in Cyprus. For this reason there is a tradition of suspicion of police powers throughout the continent, very much in contrast with the move to greater centralisation of police powers in the UK after 1964. Strangely, the UK is perceived by some European commentators to be moving away from the features of British policing that make it most attractive. It is odd that the UK appears to be centralising at a time when the rest of Europe wishes to adopt more of the Anglo Saxon elements of policing as described in the previous section (see Chapter 5).

Although the Spanish and Portuguese experiences could be characterised as modernised authoritarianism rather than totalitarianism, and the Greeks under the colonels in the late 1960s and early 1970s suffered similarly, civilianising, democratising and decentralising police power became priorities for these countries along with the rest of continental Europe. Ireland, of course, having emerged from the colonial experience in 1922, also has had to change its policing organisation dramatically this century.

England, Wales, Scotland, Northern Ireland and Sweden stand alone as escaping totalitarianism, authoritarianism or colonialism and there are those who would exclude Northern Ireland from that list. England and Wales constituted the only countries to reduce the number of police organisations until the Greek reform of 1984 and the Dutch reform of the early 1990s.

The Influence of Violence on Policing Systems

Violence can change the priority tasks of the organisation and the way in which it is organised. Terrorism has had an impact on policing in Northern Ireland, Germany,

Italy and Spain. Yet it was not really terrorism, but rioting and the collapse of police legitimacy that caused dramatic changes to the Royal Ulster Constabulary (RUC). Until 1969, the RUC was a relatively small force, with a reserve for public disorder, the 'B-Specials'. The failure of these two organisations to handle marches demanding Civil Rights, and then to deal even-handedly with intercommunal rioting, led to the disbandment of the B-Specials, the confinement of the RUC to barracks and the introduction of the Army on the streets of Belfast and other towns. Since then the RUC has expanded and been completely reorganised. It is now a thoroughly professional force, but still has to win back the consent of the Catholic ghettos. Its officers have been attacked by Protestant mobs, but it still faces problems in keeping the peace when the communities wish to march or riot.

The Spanish experience possibly provides a parallel in terms of the problem, but not in terms of the solution. ETA, the Basque terrorist group, mostly laid down its arms after the creation of the Autonomous Communities. The restoration of any legitimacy to the Guardia Civil was seen as impossible, so the new Basque administration created a new police, with bright red uniforms and berets. Between 1986 and 1996, it took over the policing of the Basque country, beginning in the country districts and finally replacing the municipal police in Bilbao, San Sebastian and Vitoria-Gasteiz. The Guardia Civil is still responsible for any policing role of a military type, which includes border control and cross-border cooperation. Unfortunately, though much reduced in size, ETA continues to operate and the Ertzaintza still has to cope with disorder.

The German experience with the Red Army Fraktion transformed German policing, at least to the extent of making money available for training and buildings. At Borken, visited as part of a study tour, the police station is totally integrated with the rest of local government services in a single building complex. The Polizei Führungs Akademie (PFA) is an astonishing building and worth contrasting with Bramshill in England, which is a curious mixture of mediaevalism and a regimental mess. The modernism of the art and architecture at Münster, the spaciousness of the individual en-suite student rooms and the central café bar are appropriate to the Europe of the 1990s in a way in which many police buildings across Europe are not. The Germans have always had the BGS to deal with public disorder and when this becomes wide-scale, the police academy students have always been used as a reserve public order force.

Disorderly crowds, and fighting with the police during a demonstration or even a night out drinking, are more common in the UK than they used to be, and riot training, together with a different 'uniform' and appearance, has become part of the UK police experience since 1980. This is not necessarily true for all constabularies, although it is for Greater Manchester Police and the Metropolitan Police. The amount of violence in a society will clearly influence the degree of discipline and technology required of the police and will consequently influence the amount of involvement with the Army, as well as the degree to which a police organisation is truly civilian or paramilitary. Unlike the UK, Spain and Germany, France has, in the CRS, a rare force purely designed for confronting crowds and demonstrations.

To summarise, because the police have the task of enforcing the laws promulgated by the state, where there have been violent changes in a country in which the population has suffered, there has been corresponding suspicion of the sheer extent and power of the police. As a result, there has been some interest in preventing it from being able to pursue its role as an arm of the state so wholeheartedly again.

The experience of violence outside wartime has been one justification for the continuation of paramilitary forms of policing, although in democratic systems the impact this has upon police legitimacy is the subject of debate and police action can lead to alienation of the wider public. Accordingly, retraining, not only in crowd management techniques but also in how to deal with the public, has entered the list of police managers' concerns (see Chapters 4 and 5).

Police Tasks

The problem of policing disorder will be examined in more detail in Chapter 3. For now, it serves as a reminder that policing involves not only crime management (*repression*) but also order maintenance (*prevention; ordre public*). These are generally considered to be the 'core tasks' of policing. Examples of crime management and order maintenance tasks are listed below. To these can be added peripheral tasks that may or may not have been allocated to organisations bearing the title 'police':

It is worth noting that a survey carried out for the Ertzaintza (Basque police) identified 350 different tasks involved in the police function, so the items on the list above can only be taken as examples of police work. The common feature is 'preventive patrol', the raison d'être of the New Police of 1829 (Reith, 1956). What was required was a body of men who could be employed to patrol the streets to prevent crime and small-scale disorder, who could also be used as a disciplined body to meet large-scale disorder without the need to deploy lethal force, with its concomitant risk of causing public disaffection. Hence policing in England and Wales, from 1829 onwards, involved the primary functions of crime management and order maintenance, in all senses of the phrase, but it shared aspects of these functions with other institutions such as the yeomanry, the militia, the courts and politicians at both local and national level.

Crime Management	Order Maintenance	Peripheral Tasks
preventive patrol	preventive patrol	traffic management
receive reports of crime	crowd management	firearms licensing
investigate crime	surveillance of popular mood	private security licensing
prosecute offenders	Respond flexibly and appropriately	prevention of desertion from the battlefield
maintain cells		emergency response

Core and Peripheral Tasks of Policing

Policing Structures and Systems

There is a British myth that all Continental European police services are single, national organisations. As demonstrated in Chapter I (Tables II-V), whilst Denmark, Finland and Ireland do have a single, unified, national force, most European countries have competing organisations, one or more of which may be centralised. They may exist in competition with locally organised services, or be restricted to a specific role or the enforcement of a specific set of

	Mission	Municipal Force Gemeentepolitie	State Police Rijkspolitie
Overall responsibility	Maintaining order	Burgomeister	Ministry of Interior
Overall responsibility	Law enforcement	Public prosecutor	Public prosecutor
Management		Burgomeister	Ministry of Justice
Where?		Towns over 25,000	Rural areas

Table IX. Dutch Policing Before Reform

laws. Various alternatives have already been given, such as countries that have separate rural and urban systems; those federalised on the German model and those that are decentralised on a county model. Equally, sometimes there is functional differentiation that involves accountability to different ministries.

To illustrate the continental perception of policing, Table IX, which depicts Dutch policing before its recent reform, is useful and will be revisited in later chapters. This demonstrates the conception of the two core tasks of the police and the two different supervisors of each mission. Public order is a matter for the city in urban areas and the state in rural areas. Law enforcement is a judicial matter. The same officer can be performing both tasks in the course of a shift but is responsible to different authorities.

The general principles behind existing police organisational structures within the European Union reflect a conflict between order-maintenance and crime management. The monarchy and its successor, the nation state, had different security priorities to those of the emerging urban communities. The state wanted security from overthrow and therefore made order its priority, but it also had property to protect and was not indifferent to crime management. Town-dwellers wanted security from crime, against both person and property. They also had a secondary interest in preserving order, and the burghers who paid the taxes had an interest in combatting trades-unionism. Country-dwellers, however, wanted to settle their own disputes internally and to be protected against outsiders.

In many parts of Europe this led to the emergence of two totally different organisations, one paid for by local taxes and responsible to town government; the other paid for by national taxes and responsible to national government. In some countries this is further complicated by the existence of provincial administrations at an intermediate geographical level; even England has counties, not to mention Scotland and Ireland. Germany, Italy, Belgium and to some degree, Spain, were and are not really nation states, in the sense that a single ethnic group with a single religion and language is overwhelmingly dominant.

Both Italy and Germany were a mixture of city-states and personal fiefdoms prior to 19th century 'unification' projects and many of those more local allegiances and identifications are held today. In general, policing arrangements and paymasters were, and are, different in urban and rural areas. In the rural areas some facilities and equipment have been paid for by the Minister of the Interior, others by the Ministry of Defence, because gendarmeries played a different role according to whether there was war or peace. In the urban areas payment is partly from the city authorities and partly from the Ministry of Interior. In both rural and urban areas, investigation was and is a matter for the Ministry of Justice and permanent detective units are at least part-funded by this Ministry. Where financial crime is concerned, the Treasury or Finance Ministry will have an interest: Customs and Guardia di Finanza are centrally funded by this Ministry, because of their involvement in preventing loss of revenue.

The role of the Ministry of Defence in policing is in decline, as divided rural-urban systems are increasingly being reformed along the lines of the post-1964 England and Wales model. Similarly, conscript armies have been replaced by professional, small, hi-tech armies, who no longer require a gendarmerie to prevent desertion from the battlefield. As a result, rural, military police services are either being amalgamated with civilian, urban services, as in the Netherlands; are being civilianised as in Belgium and Portugal; or, as in Spain, autonomous communities are being given a choice between continuing with the existing system of municipal police (de ayuntamiento) plus paramilitaries, or setting up their own unified all-community police services, as have the Basques and the Catalans.

Overall, change is underway and the military elements in policing are disappearing. However, the differentiation between the interests of the local community and those of the state tend to remain in the division of policing units into those who primarily deal with local crime and those who maintain order. This is overlaid by differences in the organisation of policing in rural and urban areas. Political and financial control and accountability are recurrent issues.

Conclusion

Many different interests have been identified in this chapter. Some police organisations police on behalf of the state or the government. Others will police for the local community, although the greater the percentage of their funding provided by central government, the more the latter will expect its priorities to be followed.

The major differences between European police services have been identified as lying in their structure, their powers, the form of their political and judicial accountability and their financial accountability. Uniformity exists in that similar tasks are undertaken by all the police organisations, whether they be performed under one unified national system; separate rural and urban systems; according to functional differentiation or omnicompetence; in a decentralised county or a federalised model; by the only system available or by competing systems in the same territory.

The next two chapters focus on the two core police missions of crime management/law-enforcement and order maintenance, in the course of which discretion, political and judicial accountability and the more obvious organisational problems will be discussed.

3. Repression

Introduction

In continental Europe policing is commonly divided into two different missions, 'repression' and 'prevention'. This chapter focuses on the first of these. The mission of repression is concerned with crime: its detection, investigation and prosecution. Three main elements run through this chapter. These are the role of the detective or investigator; the system of laws under which crimes and their sentences are defined; and the judicial system, which directs how crimes and criminals may be investigated and brought to trial. Consequent upon these, each country also has organisational procedures, which determine how, and to whom, an investigation should be assigned and how it should be overseen in order to satisfy legal and judicial requirements.

Issues in the Development of the Detective Role

Every police force and service in Europe recognises that the investigation of crime requires particular skills; there are specialist organisations that deal with crime rather than routine patrol. Whereas many of the policing roles discussed in Chapter 1 go back some centuries, the idea that detection is a specific role that should be performed by officers dedicated to this task is of comparatively recent origin.

It was at the turn of the 19th century that European governments saw the need to formalise policing itself into an organisation separate from the military. Because detectives were already being employed in semi-private organisations their introduction into the police was not without its problems. This private employment and their closeness to the criminals they were tasked to catch raised questions about their allegiance and their probity; questions which in one form or another are still raised today and which are expanded below.[1]

Prior to the creation of the ' New Police' in London in 1829 criminal investigation had been very much neglected. Making enquiries into the circumstances of a crime and collecting information with a view to tracing and prosecuting the criminal were unnecessary in rural communities, where everyone knew everyone else. As a result large numbers of private prosecution societies had come into existence to perform what should have been the duty of the police.

The Bow Street Runners were the best known example of such private organisations, although the individuals who founded it had held the office of constable under the old system. They took up a case if, and when, sufficient remuneration seemed likely. They were normally eight in number and were available to the highest bidder for their services in any part of the country; receiving a retainer of a guinea a week. They were not immediately incorporated into the new Metropolitan Police and continued in existence from 1829 to 1839. They were initially unpopular and were called 'thieftakers', which appears to have the same connotations as the term 'bounty-hunters'.

The new Metropolitan Police had the responsibility to institute an investigation immediately a crime was reported, whether or not an individual came forward to prosecute or meet the cost of enquiries. It was handicapped partly by the view that 'Thief taking or thief catching was looked upon as a peculiar craft or art or mystery requiring long years of initiation as well as special aptitude', (Moylan, 1934: 178), and by the fact that Sir Richard Burney, Chief Magistrate of Bow Street, and his colleagues, tried as far as possible to grant warrants only to his own officers.[2] This element of competition and staking claims can still be seen today, for example in the competition between the Gendarmerie and Police Municipale in Belgium. It was also considered that the creation of a new detective police was politically unacceptable and would have been denounced as involving espionage and as an imitation of foreign methods, particularly those of the French under the Ancien Régime and Napoleon.

The political implications of a centralised, government-controlled police organisation, a possible threat to democracy, have long constituted an obstacle to the creation of a national police organisation in the UK. When reviewing the organisational structure of the police, the Royal Commission of 1962, although considering a national detective agency desirable, decided that it was politically unacceptable and recommended regional organisation instead (Royal Commission, 1962). Although there is now a National Criminal Intelligence Service (NCIS) in the UK, this follows the Dutch model of the CRI, which collates and analyses information but leaves operational matters to the individual local organisations. An operational arm, the National Crime Squad, was established in 1997, after it became clear that NCIS was having difficulty with Chief Constables and Regional Crime Squad heads over resources. New systems of financial accountability and budgetary independence were at the heart of NCIS's problems. Without its own operational arm, any attempt to use another organisation's officers involved the effective usurpation of that organisation's budget.

Political accountability has always been seen as being of greater importance than judicial accountability in England and Wales, although the Continental model, which involves the judiciary in the oversight of investigation, is followed in Scotland where the procurator fiscal plays this role. The issue of accountability is one that runs throughout the historic and contemporary deployment of detectives and will be returned to later in this chapter.

A semi-official detective corps had come into existence in Paris in 1810 when Vidocq, an ex-criminal-turned-police agent, organised other criminals or ex-criminals into the Brigade de Sûreté who informed against their old associates and had a reputation for arranging or instigating many of the crimes they detected. The Bow Street Runners, though not ex-criminals, also associated with the criminal classes in the 'flash houses'. This was forbidden to the new constables of the Metropolitan Police. This is another major issue. Detectives today argue that professional criminals are always planning jobs and that to catch them at the scene of the crime offers a better opportunity of a conviction than an investigation after the crime has been committed;

association with criminals is the only way to do this. Similarly, information from one criminal is needed to catch another, and so it becomes important to build up relationships with the professional criminals. Sometimes, however, this can lead to corruption (Moylan, 1934: 185)[3], and does lead to conflict of interest and to questions about the legality of entrapment.

The ways in which different countries have come to terms with this problem are closely related to the various organisational structures of criminal investigation work, which in turn have much to do with the criminal justice system and the form of judicial accountability under which they operate. Political fears are also associated with the wearing of plain clothes by detectives when the rest of the police wear uniform. This can be presented as espionage. Indeed, Moylan reports that in 1868-69 Scotland Yard was sensitive to accusations of espionage and therefore refused to employ non-police officers on detective work. Undercover work is the modern equivalent of espionage and raises the problem that the undercover officer can sometimes be party to a criminal act. In addition, such an officer can be accused of acting as an agent provocateur.

Even if undercover work can be defended as legitimate for the apprehension of a criminal, it is more problematic when political organisations are penetrated by plain-clothes police officers. Nineteenth-century officers such as Popjay were dismissed for this. The tactics employed against the post-1968 terrorist movements of Western Europe have raised the issue again. The arguments involved are the same as those concerning the suspension of human rights in times of national emergency. The same tactics are now being introduced against organised crime and raise the same dilemmas.

Most countries try to circumvent these problems by creating what is in effect a 'political' police or an anti-subversive police, for example the German Office for the Preservation of the Constitution [BfV] and the British Special Branch. These organisations are accountable to political authorities by routes quite different to those for the mainstream detective branch. Equally most countries go through periods when the government of the day can be accused of misuse of the police investigative function in a drive against political opponents. In the UK, for example, there is still controversy over the use of the police during the Miners' Strike of 1984-85. In Germany, police tactics against student demonstrators in the late 1960s and early 1970s have been held responsible by some commentators for the rise of the Baader-Meinhof terrorists. In Italy, controversy still rages over the role of the intelligence services in the events of the late 1960s and early 1970s.

To concern about the relationship between investigation and political and judicial accountability can be added the issue of internal oversight of investigation within the police. This is not new. In 1878 it was laid down that, whilst detectives carried out their work under the instruction of their superior officers in the CID, their reports would pass through the divisional superintendent of the police 'so as to preserve his general responsibility for all the police in his division.' (Moylan, 1934: 187). Failures in internal accountability and oversight have led to major causes célèbres: cases such as the Birmingham Six and the Maguire Seven involved forensic failures as well as abuses of human rights and interrogation procedure. The relationship between detectives and informants has also been a source of concern, leading to the instigation of informant handling rules. Nevertheless, immunity from prosecution proffered to informants continues to be subject to judicial challenge in the courts.

In summary, the development of detection as a specialist role has raised fears about the potential for such skills to be abused. This abuse has been by the government against the populace or specific groups within it; by the police themselves in pursuit of convictions and an improved clear-up rate and by individual officers using their skills and contacts in 'private' and corrupt enterprise. A variety of institutional methods have been adopted to attempt to control the activities of detectives, ranging from organisational rules of procedure to structures of political and judicial accountability.

Reporting a Crime

The majority of crime reports are received over the telephone in a control room as a result of an emergency call by a member of the public: the beginning of most crime investigation lies in that decision to ring the police. In the UK the number called is 999; however 911 is supposed to become the general number for emergency calls throughout the EU. In a number of countries, unlike the UK, the citizen has to decide which police to call. Historically a Belgian citizen had to decide whether to call the Gendarmerie or the Police Municipale. An Italian is still faced with a decision as to whether to call the Carabinieri, the Urbani or the Vigile. In some countries the police compete to be assigned an investigation and calls can go to individual police stations which have their own emergency number. However the emergency number called is most frequently routed to a police control room where the details of the call are taken and decisions made as to what action to take. The number and distribution of control rooms varies: they may be centralised for a whole force area or dedicated to a specific geographic area or types of event; they may be solely for police; for police and fire services or for all emergency services; they may be permanent or temporary. Paris, for example, has a control room for traffic and public disorder. The Hague in the Netherlands has a normal control room and an emergency control room which is used on occasions when there are major demonstrations or major crowd control movements, so that the normal policing of the city is not disturbed. In the UK, control rooms can be set up temporarily at events such as the Henley Regatta where movements of large numbers of people need to be overseen.

But control rooms are becoming increasingly standardised. Most will have a board showing the location of the various motorised units available to the 'dispatchers' who will be sitting in front of VDUs on which they can record the number of the caller and can look to see the last reported position of foot patrol officers and cars. Most will also have a tape running to record the content and time of calls. This provides information such as the time taken to answer a call and the speed with which a unit is despatched, and is a means of assessing procedures and decisions taken in particular cases. There is still discussion in police services as to whether a single centralised control room or a mixture of centralised and local control rooms is the best way of dealing with incoming calls. The problem lies in deciding what goes to the central control room and what stays locally.

Control rooms vary in their way of working. A constabulary in the UK may have one or several. In many UK control rooms the operator is a civilian. This is unusual in the rest of Europe, where an operator is usually in uniform, possessed of police powers and has a police rank. The calls coming in on the emergency number are not necessarily crime-related; many are requests for information and assistance, which come to the police as the 'only 24-hour social service'. To separate these from calls which may require immediate action, a screening process has been instituted in many forces. On the basis of the seriousness of the crime and the demands already being made on the personnel available, the dispatcher will take a decision as to whether immediate response is required or even possible.

The nature of the caller and the place from which the call originates may also make a difference. For example, in the UK, a call about a problem on the railways would be passed to the British Transport Police. If in doubt, or if the call raises the likelihood that specialist units may be required, a uniformed officer will be at hand to take relevant decisions. Furthermore, there will be an officer of at least Inspector rank in overall charge of the control room, where this is an all-constabulary facility. An officer may be dispatched to the scene and may deal with the situation personally or may radio back to the control room if further personnel are required. The officer will decide whether an offence has been committed. If so, in the UK the officer may decide to exercise discretion, in the sense that the officer will not make an arrest but simply issue a warning as to future behaviour. In some countries there is no such decision to be made; for example in Germany officers have no discretion in such matters. In this country the officer will further decide to fill in a report form or bring the situation to the attention of an officer of higher rank for decision. Decisions taken at this level will affect the recorded crime figures quite dramatically, and reflect the priorities of any case-screening system. They will also reflect the priorities of the custody officer as discussed below.

In many European countries, the officer receiving the call will not only have to take a decision as to whether an immediate response is required, but also will have to decide whether to alert the judicial authorities as well as the appropriate branch of police investigation. The judicial authority will then take a decision as to which organisation will handle the investigation after seeing the scene of the crime and personally interviewing appropriate witnesses. The relationship between the investigating police officer in charge and the judicial authority will vary greatly and depend upon personality and political party membership.

If the offence is seen as trivial, the callers may simply be asked to present themselves at the station to fill in the report form themselves. This is most likely to be the case when a minor burglary has occurred. Case screening is not as common on the continent as it is in the UK. In the UK in cases of burglary or report of a theft, the first decision is taken on the basis of the monetary value concerned. If this is under £500 the events of the crime will simply be recorded. If it is between £500 and £1000 a report will be made to CID. A value of over £1000 will lead to a decision to despatch appropriate personnel. This decision is mitigated by the nature of the victim. For example, elderly victims will receive a visit from the police as will other categories seen as 'sensitive', in other words, where the media are likely to castigate the police if they fail to make a visit to the victim.

If physical evidence is to be gathered for analysis, or the environmental factors affecting the commission of the crime may need to be used in evidence, a decision may be taken to call in the Scene of Crime Officers (SOCOs). These may be specially trained constables or, as in the UK, civilians. An appropriate Forensic Science Service, which may be under the control of the police, the Ministry of Justice or even privately owned, will make analysis of such evidence, but a decision will have to be taken as to whether it is appropriate to spend funds in a particular case. Such decisions may also be made during the course of the investigation, by whichever body holds the prosecutorial role. In the UK this is the Crown Prosecution Service; in other systems the juge d'instruction or procurator can make decisions as to whether to proceed further with a case.

Types and Levels of Crime

In many European countries, especially those following the French model, there is a clear distinction between minor crime (*delit* in French) and major crime (*crime*). The criterion used is usually that of sentence length: if the maximum sentence is 3 years, or sometimes 5 years, the crime is minor. A delit, which once probably would have been translated as a 'misdemeanour' in the UK, is a matter for the uniform branch. A crime is a matter for the detective branch. In Belgium the investigation of a minor offence will also be a matter for a juge d'instruction. A major offence will be a matter for the procurator.

Thus the institution placed in charge of the investigation of crime reflects the level of court and judicial proceeding involved, which in turn reflects the penalty involved. In its turn this is a result of the perception of the seriousness of the offence. The Spanish define *delitos* as serious offences that involve more than six years in prison. *Faltas* are the petty offences. Faltas are investigated by the investigating judge (the Juez de Instruccion), except where the crime is extremely minor, and is dealt with by the justice of the peace of the place in which the offence was committed. Delitos carrying a penalty of six years imprisonment or less are judged by the investigating judge. Serious delitos, those carrying a penalty of over six years imprisonment, are judged by the provincial court of justice. The similar dividing line in France is five years between a delit and crime. The system in England and Wales used to be divided between felonies and misdemeanours, but is now between offences and serious arrestable offences, as defined by the Criminal Justice Act of 1985. In England and Wales different courts may deal with different levels of offence, but this does not affect the supervision of the investigation. In Belgium, France, Spain, Luxembourg and maybe one or two other countries, the severity of the offence affects the officer carrying out the investigation, sometimes the authority supervising the investigation and even the powers of the officer carrying out the investigation. The relative importance of the official, other than a police officer, supervising the investigation appears to reflect the need for the exercise of certain police powers to be authorised by somebody other than a police officer. Thus officials with varying levels of judicial authority are empowered in different countries to authorise impositions on freedom such as searching of property and detention.

Taking Portugal as a model rather than the UK,[4] criminal proceedings begin with the reporting of the crime, which can either be done by the public prosecutor, by the police, by a public body, or by a private individual. This report goes to the public prosecutor (PP). The PP then opens an enquiry, which the PP directs assisted by the police. A judge can intervene, although normally the public prosecutor is in charge of this phase of procedure. Only a judge can order acts which can affect rights, freedoms and guarantees protected by the constitution. Thus parliament has removed the exercise of certain acts from the jurisdiction of the public prosecutor, e.g. the interrogation of an arrested person, searches and seizures in lawyers' offices, doctors' surgeries or banking establishments. Parliament has also conferred certain measures to the exclusive jurisdiction of the investigating judge, e.g. search of dwellings, seizure of correspondence and listening to, or recording of, conversations or telephone calls.

The enquiry phase is closed by a decision to present the indictment or to shelve the case. This depends on whether the public prosecutor has gathered enough evidence to establish the commission of a crime and to identify a potential suspect. This decision can be confirmed by a phase called 'instruction' or a preliminary judicial investigation. This comes within the jurisdiction of a judge (juiz de instrucao). Either the accused or the victim can move for an 'instruction' phase. This is intended as a judicial corroboration of the public prosecutor's decision either to file an indictment or to drop the case. This phase ends with a decision whether or not to proceed to trial. It is not a necessary phase, for the public prosecutor may have already taken the decision to move forward with the trial and it may not have been opposed by the accused. This system is therefore divided into the reporting of the crime, the investigation, the indictment or the abandonment of the case or the review of the decision to indict or to abandon and then finally the trial.

Other systems have a pre-trial review phase as well. The type and level of a crime affect investigation greatly, as does whether or not there is a case screening system, under which crimes that do not fit the criteria for investigation are simply dealt with by interviewing the person reporting the crime and completing a crime report. Case screening is usually used for minor crimes of which there are a great many, in which the monetary value of the loss from theft or burglary is below a set limit, there is little physical evidence by which to identify the perpetrator and the chances of detection are correspondingly low. Case screening, in other words, reflects the impact of restricted resources on the police, rather than the impact of a crime on the victim.

Some UK forces have adopted a 'crime desk' system to facilitate the initial reporting of crime. Some use it also for coordinating all the processes of mounting an investigation, as the Association of Chief Police Officers, Her Majesty's Inspectorate of Constabulary and the Audit Commission suggest is good practice:

> Effective crime management requires an appropriate and efficient initial response; prompt identification of cases meriting further investigation by detectives; integration of investigation, intelligence and scientific support inputs; and a high quality of communication with victims of crime. This represents a substantial task of co-ordination

and progress monitoring, and a number of forces have adopted the crime desk mechanism to undertake it. (ACPO, HMIC and Audit Commission, 1994)

Another variable that must be taken into account is the type of crime being investigated. For example, in most countries fraud is increasingly seen as a crime requiring a specialist approach, given the complexities involved in demonstrating that an offence has been committed. It is becoming more common for multi-agency groups involving police officers, prosecutors, accountants and lawyers to work together on a case. Italy has long had a Guardia di Finanza to handle such crimes. The UK has a number of competing groups: the Serious Fraud Office, the Department of Trade and Industry, and regional and local Fraud Squads. As discussed in a later chapter, the European Commission's own anti-fraud unit UCLAF is trying to convince all member states to create a single unit to coordinate fraud investigation because of the increasingly cross-border nature of the crime.

Drug crime is another area that most countries deal with in a specialist manner. Smuggling may be left to Customs to deal with, but drug-taking and dealing are matters for specialist prevention and enforcement squads. Vice has also been the province of specialist units. The expansion of car theft is another area that has led to a specialist response.

The danger of setting up specialist squads is that the big picture can easily be lost. Resources can be taken from lesser crimes, which may in fact be more numerous, though less interesting to the media. It can also encourage a perception amongst detectives that career advancement involves getting into specialist work.

Responsibilities in Crime Investigation

A number of decision points in the process of beginning an investigation are similar across the countries of the EU. The major differences lie in who has the responsibility for various aspects of investigation and these are summarised in Table X.

Table X demonstrates that there are basically 3 models of investigative accountability. The key variable is who supervises investigation. Under the English model the police themselves supervise their investigation. The prosecutor is in overall charge in the German model and in the French model it is a judge, sometimes called an examining magistrate, who is in charge. The English model is that followed in England, Wales, Ireland and Denmark. Details were not available in van den Wyngaert (see Note 5) for Sweden and Finland, but a telephone interview with a Swedish Chief Prosecutor suggested that both follow the German model. France, Belgium, Luxembourg and Spain are systems where the judge is in charge. Italy has recently changed from a judge to a prosecutor. Belgium and Spain actually have a hybrid system depending upon the seriousness of the offence being investigated. Scotland, Germany the Netherlands and now, Italy, can be placed in the German model.

Although the Table may suggest uniformity of practice in countries with similar systems, there are considerable national differences in the way the systems are implemented. Though the judge or the prosecutor may be said to be in general charge of an investigation, in fact it is mostly the police who do the work. The degree to which

Country	Who investigates minor crime?	Who investigates major crime?	Who supervises investigation?	Who Prosecutes?
Belgium	PJ[a] & Prosecutor	PJ & Judge	Prosecutor/Judge	Prosecutor
Denmark	Police	Police	Police	Chief of Police or Prosecutor
England & Wales	Police	CID	Police	Prosecutor
France	PJ (agents)	PJ (officers)	Judge	Prosecutor
Germany	Schutzpolitzei	Kripo[b]/BKA[c]	Prosecutor	Prosecutor
Greece	Police	Judge	Police	Prosecutor
Ireland	Police	Police	Police	Police/Prosecutor
Italy	Police	PJ	Public Prosecutor	Prosecutor
Luxembourg	PJ	PJ	Judge after formal enquiry open	Prosecutor
Netherlands	Police	Police/ Prosecutor	Prosecutor	Prosecutor
Portugal	PJ & Criminal Police	PJ & Criminal Police	Prosecutor	Prosecutor
Scotland	Police	Procurator Fiscal	Procurator Fiscal	Procurator Fiscal
Spain	PJ	PJ	Prosecutor or Investigating Judge	Prosecutor

Table X. Responsibilities in investigation in the EU[5]
a   Judicial Police
b   Kriminalpolizei
c   Bundeskriminalamt

judges and prosecutors intervene has more to do with the personalities and political ambitions of the individuals involved than to the regular nature of the system. In most cases the supervision of the investigation is a purely formal role and the police concerned are very much left to get on with the business of collecting evidence. A wise police officer, however, will consult the judge or prosecutor at appropriate points when decisions need to be taken that will have implications for the trial process itself.

Another aspect of the Table worthy of comment is the presence of the PJ (Judicial Police). In Spain all officers are also officers of the PJ when performing their investigative role. In most of the other countries with a Judicial Police all officers can be PJ in certain circumstances and there are only small numbers of individuals who are permanently employed in a PJ role. The actual numbers of officers in France or Belgium, for example, is quite small. In France, the PJ are divided into Officers (OPJ) and Agents (APJ). OPJ can conduct investigations, carry out searches and seizures and detain for up to 24 hours. APJ can draw up official records and record statements of individuals but do not have the authority to detain a person in custody. Both may breathalyse people. The PJ is not quite the same sort of animal as the CID in England and Wales or the Kripo and the BKA in Germany. These organisations are staffed by full-time officers performing a detective role with their own career structures and notions of professionalism.

The notion that a judicial officer is supervising the investigation is not wholly correct in practice. It reflects a conviction in the countries concerned that the exercise of police powers to invade privacy or to restrict freedom is best authorised by a judicial authority and that someone other than the police should have oversight of the investigation and should be concerned with reviewing the evidence to establish the truth. There is a perceived danger that the police become partisan in the course of an investigation and seek to prove their case having decided upon the suspect, rather than establish whether the suspect concerned is actually responsible for the offence. This reflects the difference between the inquisitorial and adversarial systems. In the adversarial system, the prosecution and defence are supposed to be advocates making the best possible case for their client. The judge or the jury or both decide whether to convict on the basis of the case presented to them. In the inquisitorial system, the prosecutor and/or judge are supposed to be more concerned with establishing the truth of the situation and supposedly play a completely neutral role in examining the evidence.

In practice, most systems in Europe now mix adversarial and inquisitorial aspects. Nevertheless, the role of the prosecutor is defined differently in a variety of systems. In Denmark, for example, the police gather evidence, irrespective of whether it be for the prosecution or the defence. Full simultaneous discovery of the results of police investigations is made to both defence and prosecution. The police normally can be asked to undertake particular enquiries by the defence as well as by the prosecution. The local chief-of-police is supposed to act, not as an agent of the government, but as an objective decision-maker, examining the evidence before deciding whether it is sufficient for a prosecution. The prosecutor deals only with the most serious cases.

A number of recent decisions made by the European Court of Human Rights have affected all European criminal investigations. Telephone tapping, and other invasions of privacy have consequently been declared illegal by such countries as Belgium. It is legal, however, to submit as evidence a phone number called from a number being investigated. Elsewhere the assumption that a judge both could, and should, be the authority who permits invasions of privacy when a request is made by the investigative institutions, is under reconsideration. Decisions of the European Court of Human Rights are producing convergence in periods for which an accused person can be detained without being brought before the judge and other exercisers of police power. Though there are many obstacles to the organisation of criminal procedures throughout the EC, decisions of the European Court of Human Rights and, since the signing of the Treaty of Amsterdam, the European Court of Justice, are pushing legal systems towards convergence.

country	1990	1991	1992	1993	1994
Austria	457623	468832	502440	493786	504568
Belgium					577902
Denmark	527416	519735	536827	546914	546928
Finland	437700	391671	392872	387244	389287
France	3492712	3744112	3830996	3881894	3919008
Germany					
Greece	330803	358998	379652	358503	303311
Ireland					
Italy	2501640	2647737	2390539	2259903	2173448
Luxembourg		15787	18077	19452	21067
Netherlands					
Portugal					
Spain	826031	795291	738781	736160	692915
Sweden	1218812	1199101	1195154	1191251	1112505
England & Wales	4543611	5276173	5591717	5526255	5249478
Northern Ireland	57198	63492	67532	66228	67886
Scotland	535864	592774	589562	543013	527064

Table XI. Total recorded crime in the EU 1990-94 (Source: UN)

Comparative Criminal Statistics

As already noted, criminologists disagree passionately as to whether anything can be concluded from statistics, given that the way they are gathered varies from country to country and from year to year. The following statistics in Table XI have been included to show the sort of workload involved in investigation.

Ireland, the Netherlands, Germany and Portugal had not made returns to the UN for any of the years concerned.

The gross statistics tell the reader very little, so Table XII presents them as crimes per 100,000 inhabitants. The Spanish figure looks incredibly low, and it is possible that only delitos have been included, and not faltos. The picture presented is certainly at odds with the prejudices of the average English tourist.

Organisations involved in criminal investigation

In the UK the Police and Criminal Justice Act of 1984 forms a watershed. Before that date the police prosecuted most minor crime. Going back a little further a distinction would have been drawn between a misdemeanour and a felony, the distinction being that, in line with the rest of Europe, misdemeanours carried a sentence of three years or less, and felonies or other levels of crime carried a higher sentence. The Magistrates'

country	crime rate
Spain	1770
Greece	2909
Italy	3800
Northern Ireland	4160
Luxembourg	5254
Belgium	5733
Austria	6283
France	6787
Finland	7641
England & Wales	10205
Scotland	10269
Denmark	10508
Sweden	12671

Table XII. Crimes per 100,000 population in the EU, 1994 (Source: UN)

Court could award a sentence of up to three years, and to get a sentence of a greater duration the case had to go to a higher level. The higher level of court would normally involve a jury, whereas at the lower level the Magistrate could decide guilt and punishment.

Since 1985 all prosecution has been carried out by the Crown Prosecution Service and the police have been removed from a role in prosecution. The Act also introduced the new concept of a 'Serious Arrestable Offence', and also the role of the 'Custody Officer' who is now responsible for what happens, and when, to someone in the cells at the police station.

It could be argued that, prior to this, a detective's role was primarily that of preparing paperwork and turning information into evidence. Detectives themselves may disagree, as they consider themselves to be skilled investigators, but research suggests this describes their true role. In the UK, since 1985-86, it has not been clear what a constable is supposed to be concerned with in terms of criminal investigation, nor are the responsibilities and duties of the detective area clear. It is unclear whether the Crown Prosecution Service has any supervisory role with regard to the conduct of an investigation. The lines of responsibility between the divisional detective, the regional crime squad, and the new national bodies such as the National Criminal Intelligence Service and its operational arm, the National Crime Squad, are equally indistinct. There have even been suggestions that the CID could be abolished and its members merged with the uniformed police to no great disadvantage.

Originally, the logic behind the demarcation of police roles was as follows. A constable was able to investigate and bring to justice the perpetrator of a crime committed in the area the officer normally patrolled, e.g. this would be a crime that took place on that beat and the victim and the instigator would be resident in that area. A detective would become involved in the investigation of a series of crimes that went beyond the beat of a particular officer. A detective would cover a greater geographical area and would be expected to have knowledge of more specialist areas of the law than a patrol constable. A detective would also be expected to bring additional skills to the investigation, such as preservation of the scene of crime for forensic purposes. The third level, in which the regional crime squad would become involved, would be a crime or a series of crimes for which evidence gathering would take place over a broader spectrum than a single constabulary area. This would involve some sort of travelling 'criminal'. The National Crime Intelligence Service is used when there is to be intelligence analysis of patterns of crime taking place over the country as a whole. Special Branch become involved when the crime is thought to be political in some way, also having a relationship with intelligence services in the investigation of the activities of foreign agents within the country. For crimes which involve the evasion of tax or duty the Customs & Excise Service are brought in. They also deal with the importing of illegal commodities such as drugs. The Immigration Service deals with illegal aliens. Thus a number of variables will affect the way in which criminal investigation is organised:

- the geographical area over which the crimes are committed;
- the complexity of the crime, particularly in regard to the presentation of evidence in court;
- the requirement for specialist investigative skills;
- the requirement for specialist technologies;
- the nature of the court in which the prosecution is to be brought;
- the role of the prosecuting authority in responsibility for the prosecution and for the conduct of the investigation as a whole;
- whether the crime involves the evasion of duty or the crossing of national boundaries.

Discretion, Crime and Legal Systems

Differences in legal systems produce variety in police investigative methods and structures. Different legal codes affect what is defined as criminal, the powers the police possess and the degree of discretion actually available to a police constable. A continuum may be drawn, on which at one end may be placed the German system, in which there is supposed to be no discretion, and on the other, the English and Irish models, where discretion is high. Between these extremes lie a number of police services which have maintained a direct entry officer class from their para-military past. Where discretion exists, the priority of some crimes will vary according to place, time and policy rather than their statutory position. A strong argument for the separate constabularies in the UK is that this enables the police to prioritise different crimes in different areas. An equally strong argument, against this, is that justice is enforced differently and that a travelling public finds that rules differ from place to place.

There are major differences between the common law traditions of England and Ireland; the Anglo-Dutch traditions of the Scottish, Dutch, German and Scandinavian systems, and the Roman law of the rest of continental Europe. There are variants within these legal systems and a second continuum could be drawn on which the two extremes would be pure common law and pure Roman law, with combinations of the two in between.

Similarly the inquisitorial and adversarial systems produce different outcomes. In the inquisitorial, the investigator, prosecutor and judge are all supposed to be trying to establish the truth as opposed to establishing guilt. Supporters of the inquisitorial system criticise the adversarial system as favouring the better advocate, and thus the better-off who can afford such an advocate. They argue that the truth goes begging in such a system. Supporters of the adversarial system argue that it gives more rights to the accused and that, in reality, the odds are heavily weighted in the inquisitorial system against any accused who gets to court.

Given the involvement of the judicial authorities in supervisory roles over investigation on the continent, the constable usually must be a great deal more careful, and thus in practice has a lot less discretion, than in the UK. A wrong decision in the UK may lead to a dressing-down by a sergeant. A wrong decision on the continent may lead to charges of neglect of duty by an enraged judge or procurator. There is thus a tendency to pass decisions upwards. This is further exacerbated by the fact that most European systems have a direct entry officer class. The constable can get involved in an 'us and them' perspective: decisions are for 'them'. The dirty work is for 'us'.

The levels of decision-making and the tendency to avoid responsibility may lead to a delay in taking a decision to call in forensically-skilled personnel. In consequence, evidence can be disturbed or destroyed and the integrity of the chain of evidence required for the purposes of trial undermined. Where police services are competing, or where the evidence trail leads from city to countryside and back again, matters can be further exacerbated. Prosecutors and judges seeking political and career advancement can also create problems in the whole system. In particular, a prosecutor or judge may delay calling in the genuinely specialised personnel of the Police Judiciaire proper until the trail has 'gone cold'. Prosecutors and judges with close relationships with the Gendarmerie are particularly prone to this and tend to be from the right wing of the political spectrum. The cities tend to have more left wing officials, who are equally pursuivant of advancement but who are accustomed to working in a larger organisation that contains clearly specialist roles; thus they are more likely to turn the case into one for the Police Judiciaire. Although this may mean losing control of the investigation to a higher authority, that authority is still likely to be based within the city concerned, unless there is rivalry between it and the capital city of the province in which both are situated. If possible, the capital city and the national level will be kept out. Rome is known as 'the Court of Fogs' where cases get lost, and trails that lead to capital cities tend to lead to political complexities that do not always give justice first priority.

In theory, in Germany there is no discretion for the constable. Decisions as to whether to arrest or caution are decisions for the procurator. This is the formal legal position, upon which lecturers at the Polizei Führungs Akademie were very insistent. Officers can indeed be reported by members of the public for not doing their duty. A police lawbook for an individual Land in Germany is an impressive document: it is about 300 pages long and covers every possible eventuality, thus trying to govern the decision-making of an officer. The Dutch are more relaxed about these decisions and the constable has a great deal more personal discretion. In general, constables on the continent soon learn which offences are considered trivial by their supervising officers, rather than by the custody officer, and will take decisions as to what work is a waste of time and what is not. In effect they will hand out informal cautions as to future behaviour, despite the fact that this is really the exercise of a judicial function and that a decision should be taken, or at least confirmed, by a judicial authority. If, however, they enter the incident on a form it may be that they will only be able to recommend caution as opposed to exercising it. The Dutch police found that every incident involved the completion by a constable of 14 different forms for different organisations. A new computerised system has expedited this process, but when a crime occurs the thought of the time to be spent filling in forms must keep the recorded crime rate down.

Finally, the question of who is reporting an offence is relevant. This chapter has concentrated upon the individual citizen, but an organisation or an individual in their occupational role may report an offence, such as an employer, a private security organisation or a concierge at a block of flats. Sometimes these actors may call in the police because they have suspicions but no evidence. Although there is a tendency for commercial organisations to try to settle matters internally, sometimes they need the expertise of the police, and this is provided for in some jurisdictions. Commercial organisations even have the right to initiate prosecutions in some European countries. The Public Prosecutor does not always have a monopoly on the court process.

Cultural Differences

Culture is a non-legal variable that has a significant impact on police investigatory function. If there is one thing upon which all academics appear to agree, it is that there is no single universally accepted definition of culture. In this context it refers to the norms of behaviour that are acceptable both to the citizenry and to the police. This includes not only the issue of what police behaviour is acceptable to the public in a variety of circumstances, but also which citizen behaviours are acceptable to the police. There are an increasing number of sub-cultures in all societies within the European Union. There is an historically dominant set of norms which has been continuously challenged since the 1960s and which various reactionary forces seek to re-assert. However there are also the norms of the new immigrant communities, those of old ethnic minorities, and now the norms of the followers of alternative lifestyles: New Age Travellers, squatters, gays and others.

One of the consequences of their ability to exercise discretion is that police officers tend to enforce laws differentially against members of these various groups. Reiner (1985) divides society along other lines, including the concept of 'police property', that is, those with whom the police feel they can do as they wish because they live outside the law. All societies have accepted rules of police behaviour and situations in which the police are allowed to mete out violence, to deprive citizens of their freedom and administer summary justice. The UK, for example, has long adhered to the bizarre notion of the 'sporting chance', which seems to mean that the middle classes should be let off in any encounter with the police.

A further variable producing different police organisational structures and patterns of behaviour is the pattern of crime in a given society. While criminologists argue about the validity of crime statistics, increases in recorded crime must by definition result in increased police workload, even if only at an administrative level. Similarly, the relative prevalence of particular types of crime will also affect police workload and, in turn, police priorities. Crime that is merely 'passing through' does not receive high priority; nor is crime by criminals against other criminals. Crime that creates citizen victims is more likely to meet a response.

Tolerance of particular activities in countries also differs. Other European countries see the Netherlands as a source of drugs, Belgium as a source of firearms and Luxembourg as a source of financial crime. These perceptions in part stem from the decriminalisation of soft drugs in the Netherlands, a loose firearms licensing system in Belgium and a tradition of banking secrecy in Luxembourg. As a result of these policies, the Dutch police do not bother to arrest Dutch citizens for possession of soft or hard drugs, although they will now arrest foreigners, the Belgians will not put much effort into investigating alleged illegal possession of firearms and the Luxembourgeois put little effort into investigating financial crime.

Similarly, the UK is seen as a source of football hooliganism and drunkenness, Denmark as the home of pornography, and Italy as the home of organised crime. However, this is not necessarily due to tolerance of all these activities in these countries.

Judicial Personnel, Caseload and Crime

Given the variation in the systems of investigative supervision, a moot point is whether there are significant differences between countries in terms of the personnel available to carry out the various roles of investigatory supervision. Equally, can any conclusions be drawn about the case load carried by police officers, magistrates and prosecutors in the various systems? The evidence is tenuous at best, but some comments are worth making. The overall surprise is that the differences in the three models of investigative supervision do not appear to be significantly reflected in the numbers of judicial or prosecutorial personnel.

Astonishingly, England and Wales have by far the largest judicial personnel, according to returns made to the UN (see Table XIII). This must mean that the returns are not being made by individual countries in the same way.

country	professional	lay
Austria	1589	
Belgium	1197	2171
Finland	929	4075
Germany	22134	
Greece	1366	
Luxembourg	107	0
Portugal	1248	0
Sweden	390	8000
England & Wales	985	30054
Northern Ireland	44	
Scotland	137	4241

Table XIII. Professional and Lay Judges and Magistrates in the EU, 1994 (Source: UN)

If Greece, for example, runs a judicial system with only 1,000 judges, then it is either very efficient or cases take a long time to get to court. It is much more likely that there is another category of judge, or even tribunal, that deals with summary offences. The absence of a return from France is a problem, but the Ministry of Justice home page on the World Wide Web claims that 60,102 Agents were budgeted for in 1997, including 6,287 Magistrates of the ordinary courts. There is no breakdown

country	prosecutors
Austria	200
Belgium	774
Denmark	386
Finland	334
Germany	5375
Greece	392
Luxembourg	27
Portugal	1015
Spain	1284
Sweden	717
England & Wales	2090
Scotland	249

Table XIV. Prosecutors in the EU, 1994 (Source:UN)

given for Juges d'Instruction, but a Guardian article on the Caroline Dickinson murder investigation (1997-98) put the number at just over 600 and made the point that the individual case load for each judge was far too high for the system to work successfully.

The figures in Table XIV suggest that countries have returned pure prosecutors and left out procurators. Given that Germany has a procurator-driven system, it would be reasonable to expect a greater number of personnel to be involved than just 2.5 times the England and Wales figure, where prosecutors have no supervisory role. The Scottish figure also seems surprisingly low.

Finally, Table XV allows comparison between the numbers of police and crimes per hundred thousand population. All figures are taken from the UN figures for 1994 and so unfortunately the police figures are suspect. The Spanish police figure is particularly unlikely, given the earlier Tables, unless a high percentage of Spanish police officers have been dismissed in the years between 1990 and 1994. A comparison with Table I in Chapter 1 demonstrates an interesting partial correlation between the number of police and the number of crimes. The more police, the less crime. Could this possibly be empirically verifiable? Certainly, Denmark and Sweden, with low police population ratios, have very high crime rates, yet the crime figures are not reliable. It is equally likely that a lower percentage of crime committed is actually recorded in countries such as Italy and Spain, which show high police numbers and low crime figures.

Conclusion

This Chapter has identified three models of investigative structure in the European Union:
- police-led, including England and Wales, together with some Scandinavian countries;
- magistrate-led, primarily France and until recently, Italy;
- prosecutor-led, including the Netherlands and Germany.

These models are competing, in the sense that under the Treaty of Amsterdam attempts are to be made to harmonise criminal justice systems throughout Europe. Italy is seen by the French as having treacherously defected to the German model, and thus strengthened the likelihood of that model triumphing. As discussed above, all three systems are perceived as having both faults and merits. None can be said to be 'best'.

country	police	population (00,000)	police per 00,000 population	crimes per 00,000 population
Austria	29474	80.3	367	6283
Belgium	34712	100.8	344	5733
Denmark	12372	52.1	238	10508
Finland	11816	51.0	232	7641
France	201696	577.5	349	6787
Greece	39934	104.3	383	2909
Italy				3800
Luxembourg		4.0		5254
Spain	50377	391.4	129	1770
Sweden	24759	88.0	282	12761
England & Wales	178336	514.4	347	10205
Northern Ireland	8493	16.3	520	4160
Scotland	18458	51.34	360	10269

Table XV. Police and crime per 00,000 population in the EU, 1994 (Source: UN)

Only research, which has not yet taken place, may be able to determine how they compare in terms of such variables as miscarriages of justice and speed of justice.

In Chapters 4 and 5 mention will be made of proposals for a European Judicial Area to deal with fraud against the European Budget. In these proposals there is an attempt to move from competition to complementation. The police gather information. The prosecutor decides whether it amounts to evidence, such that a case can be taken to trial, and a judge oversees the process to ensure that the rights of a potential accused are respected. The only missing aspect is that the judge should also be responsible for overseeing any process that involves an invasion of privacy or the deprivation of liberty that may take place in the investigative process. There is a role for each institution and no single institution should be the sole supervisor of the investigative process.

1   This account leans heavily on Sir John Moylan's *Scotland Yard and the Metropolitan Police*, London, Putnam and Co., 1934; an excellent example of an orthodox view.

2   The Criminal Investigation Department was created in March 1878.

3   In 1877 there was a great Scotland Yard scandal when three senior officers in the central office were found guilty of conspiring with a gang of swindlers to carry on fraudulent betting agencies.

4   This paragraph and that following summarise the account given by J. De Figueiredo Dias and M.J. Antunes in the chapter on Portugal in Christine van den Wyngaert (ed), *Criminal Procedure Systems in the European Community*, London, Butterworths. pp 327-8.

5   The information in this Table has been distilled by the authors from van den Wyngaert *op.cit.* Any misunderstanding of the information is the present authors' fault and should not be blamed on the authors of the individual articles in the book. The comments are the present authors'.

4. Prevention

Introduction

Prevention or order maintenance work involves both the prevention of disorder and the maintenance of public confidence in the police, the judicial system and the government. The francophone term *'ordre public'*, a large component of the mission of prevention, is now most frequently used in police circles to refer to their task in coping with public disorder but traditionally had to do with maintaining 'public health'. The police patrolled to keep a finger on the pulse of public opinion, as much as to reassure the public and to prevent crime by their presence. In this role the police were and are accountable to the political authorities, whether at local or national level. In their role of controlling public order and managing disorder, the police are acting as the visible arm of the state and, as such, public concern about the legitimacy of their acts tends to raise questions about the legitimacy of the state itself. The implications of undermining the public faith in the police and, in effect, their acquiescence to being policed, are such that various European countries have chosen to assign crowd maintenance to a separate, 'third' force of police. Thus although the policing discussed in this chapter is uniform policing, this includes both specialist and non-specialist officers.

The chapter is divided into two main sections, as the chief aspects of uniform work are patrol and crowd management. The first section deals with practical issues in patrol work, including community relations, types of patrol and the role of the control room and police station. The second section examines crowd management, from the role of the uniform police to the ways in which police crowd control is organised and concludes with a review of differences in crowd behaviour. Prevention work, especially in the context of crowd management, raises fundamental issues of legitimacy and political accountability. These are examined in greater depth in Chapter 5.

Practical Issues In Patrol

The sight of a uniform raises some response in any member of the public, whether it be a sense of security or of resentment. Which uniform provokes which response varies from country to country. Any face to face encounter with a uniformed police officer is perceived by a contemporary European citizen as threatening, even if it only involves the expectation of 'bad news'. A single officer on foot patrol is normally non-threatening, especially if the citizen is native to the country and over 30. A traffic police car is threatening. As a rule, the larger the group of police officers, the greater the threat felt. Most threatening of all is the police officer in body armour, wearing a helmet and visor and carrying a riot shield.

In most cities in the UK, a single officer on foot patrol was once a regular sight and provided a sense of security. Except in London during the period of the 'sus' by-law, which gave constables the right to stop and question individuals on suspicion that they were about to commit an offence, such patrolling police officers generally ignored members of the public, unless asked to provide information. The identity card produced a different situation on the continent; furthermore, one of the consequences of joining the Schengen Treaty is that a legal responsibility to carry identity cards is imposed upon citizens. One of the reasons citizens outside the UK and Ireland are reluctant to approach a police officer on the streets is because they may find themselves involved in an identity card check. A simple request for information may bring the individual to the attention of the police, causing the officer to examine the individual's records. Additionally, the way in which police officers choose whose papers they will ask to see has a great effect on how legitimate they are in the eyes of various groups.

The purpose of patrol

Foot patrol is the most visible aspect of police work. Most citizens of the European Union visit the other member states as tourists. All tourist centres have a small number of police officers whose job it is to walk around the area on foot, to prevent potential clashes between locals and visitors, and to deter pickpockets and muggers from turning tourists into victims. Greece, indeed, has a separate tourist police, multilingual and tasked with providing assistance to tourists. Foot patrol is, however, the one area of police work which is most under threat. This is partly because of the introduction of technologies such as personal radios and motor cars. However, public services are now subject to an accountancy-driven approach, under which concrete financial benefits must be demonstrated to result from each activity, and this has also threatened foot patrol. The traditional—and hard to measure— purpose of police foot patrol was to prevent crime by its very presence. Surveillance and intelligence functions were additional purposes. In the UK, at least, there was a third, service function to build up public confidence and police legitimacy.

All police forces and services in Europe undertake the patrol function, but the different purposes outlined above can conflict with each other. There are also myths about patrol, and some harking back to a former golden age of friendly local 'bobbies' who provided strict-but-fair summary justice. In discussing the possible purposes of patrol one must be careful to distinguish what is known of its effects from what is assumed.

What is the potential effect of having a uniformed presence on the street? By seeing an officer, it is argued, the public will be reassured that the police are doing their job. The officer, especially if patrolling on foot on a regular 'beat', can build relationships with the local inhabitants and shopowners, thus a relationship of trust will be established. This will lead to various benefits: - the police will be established as a friendly, rather than a hostile, presence; the talking-over of problems will alert the officer to local concerns and potential trouble; and information about local crime and criminals may even be passed on. According to this view, the local beat officer is not only a vital part of the intelligence-gathering function of the police, but may also be able to prevent the escalation of events into law breaking or disorder. By providing policing with a human face, the local beat officer is a vital element in helping support the local legitimacy of the police.

Types of patrol

The idealised picture presented above may be achievable, but foot patrol cannot supply rapid response to calls for assistance. Throughout Europe communities continue to press for local policing by officers who are part of that same community. However, developments in technology, restrictions on resources and rising rates of crime have required the reorganisation and relocation of police resources whilst they have opened up the possibility of new forms of patrol.

Local communities have not always appreciated the effect of these changes. For example, the police houses that once existed in each small community in England and Wales have been sold off. Rather than a local officer being available at any time, there is a local station, which may or may not be open. Contact with the police is only possible in many cases via the telephone, nor is there any guarantee of talking to a known officer. The smaller Belgian municipalities have obstructed police reform, for similar reasons. A decline in informal communication between the police and public, a move from informal 'self-policing' by communities to reliance on more formal methods and the escalation of petty misdemeanours into reported crime are claimed to be the result (Cain, 1973).

The advent of the patrol car and the technology for communication between car and police station had a direct affect on patrol. Patrol areas could be far larger, but communication with the control room, rather than interaction with the public, became the focus of communication. Response to calls for assistance was facilitated, but the possibility of immediate, 'hands on' policing, was removed.

Car patrol presents other problems. In a series of well-known experiments in Kansas City, USA (Kelling *et al.*, 1974), the organisation of patrol was varied in an attempt to provide both emergency cover and local beat patrolling. Unfortunately, no substantive difference was found in public confidence, crime recording or crime clear-up regardless of whether there were no cars, one, two or three patrolling an area. Although it was later claimed that a difference would have been found if more cars had been used, realistically, few forces could provide greater density of patrol cars on a regular basis.

Foot patrol remains, although increasingly it is focussed in some way. Often these chiefly affect how frequently a uniform officer walks the area. Other forms involve more significant differences, such as the use of a dedicated body of officers or a dedicated purpose to the patrolling. For example, at night in Paris, the Gendarmerie come out as the 'night patrol'. This is true of a number of major French cities. It is equally true in the smaller municipalities in Belgium that the police only provide a service during the daytime. The Gendarmerie takes over in the evening.

Attempts have been made to redress the decline in preventive foot patrol through community policing, in which officers do police their area, walking the beat in towns and cities. Even the 'red light' area in Amsterdam has its own community constable. However it is not clear that the police organisation really values or understands this work. When problems arise in an area local officers are not necessarily called in to mediate. In the UK, for example, after a fatal shooting in what was thought to be drug-related gang warfare in Moss Side, Manchester, there were complaints of insensitive policing by the CID. In Bradford, attempts were made by the leaders of the local Pakistani community to contact their community constable when intercommunal shooting broke out between the local Pakistani community and white youths. The attempt failed and riots resulted from what was seen as confrontational policing. In Scotland, while the community policing experiment on the Castlemilk Estate, Glasgow, has partly rebuilt relationships between police and inhabitants, community officers complain that when there is suspicion of a crime, detectives come in and interrogate rather than allowing them to talk to suspects, thereby undoing their work. Less sensationally, research has shown that community officers are commonly called off their beats to make up shortfalls in police strength, and that community policing is not seen by officers themselves as a role to aspire to, lacking career structure and respect from other officers.

Because there are frequent public demands for restoration of regular foot patrols by uniformed officers, various ways of providing such a presence have been tried. The unit beat system, introduced in England and Wales, rapidly collapsed under the pressure of demand from the control room. Some constabularies in England and Wales experimented with 12-hour shifts in which 8 hours were devoted to response time and 4 to pro-active policing or preventive patrol. When the new Basque police was organised it was the unit beat system that they tried to introduce, successfully in the rural areas. It proved much more difficult to install in the urban areas, where there was a high level of demand from the public via the telephone. In recent years the Devon and Cornwall Constabulary in England has experimented with a series of 'focused' patrols, in which a group of community-based officers undertake foot patrol as a preventive measure against individual crimes such as car vandalism. Where there have been a number of reports of vandalism from cars, the police will institute a sporadic night patrol as a preventive measure. There have been other experiments in patrol, for example, in Skelmersdale, England an attempt was made to combine foot patrols with a backup car patrol for emergency response (Weatheritt, 1983). Evaluation of this experiment was hampered by the lack of 'base line' data against which to compare reports of crime, contacts with the public and local clear-up rates during the initiative. Participating officers were also confused about correct procedures during the experiment, when officers were diverted from their assigned tasks to other police duties. Primary factors in the effectiveness of patrols appear to be the ways in which they are organised and manpower assigned: - neither foot nor car patrol is intrinsically better or more effective than the other.

Attempts to monitor the effectiveness of patrol have led to such initiatives as Total Geographic Policing, team policing and sector policing. All are attempts to combine intelligence gathering, crime clear-up and reassurance of the public with effective use of resources. The problem with foot patrol is that it is very difficult to measure its effect. How is it possible to demonstrate whether it prevents crime? Research by Trojanowcz in Flint, Michigan, USA (1990), indicates that, unlike motor patrol, foot patrol does have an effect on crime in the area, but that there is no difference between having one, two, three or four foot patrols. Indeed the greatest effect proved to be upon public fear of crime. The work of car patrolling officers is easier to measure, simply in terms of the speed of the response to calls from the control room. This can be used to justify the cost. Unfortunately, perhaps, whenever the financial screws are turned, it is the less measurable aspects of policing that suffer. It is hard to assess the effect that teams of dedicated beat officers have on preventing potential crime or to put a monetary value on the role they may play in avoiding major public unrest.

To satisfy demands for effectiveness, targeted patrol is increasingly used. This may be focussed on perpetrators or on crime hot spots. It shares with ordinary foot and car patrol the fact that the kind of crime it may deter is likely to be that which takes place in public—street theft and violence—rather than crimes which take place indoors and out of sight. Recently hand-held video recorders have been used to film known pickpockets and thieves in public, to let it be known that their description is on film and they could be identified if they commit a crime. This appears to be a more effective use of officers on foot than ordinary foot patrol, for the effect of the latter appears to be slight, whether on deterrence or on detection. Research has indicated that once in eight years, a police officer might intercept a criminal in the process of breaking into a property.

Supervision of patrol has always been a problem for police organisations and led to the early establishment of the police box containing a telephone for the police officer to use to report in when he/she had reached that point on the beat. Interestingly, German-style rural community policing involves the constable in the car using the car radio to report in when he or she arrives at each of a series of fixed points. Indeed, this may be one reason for the popularity of car patrol with police management; they know where officers are all the time.

The popularity of foot patrol and continued belief in its efficacy are illustrated by the significant inroads made by private policing in this area. Commercial enterprises in city centres are prepared to pay for the presence of someone in uniform who will patrol a large shop or the areas of a shopping centre. Similarly residents on housing estates have been prepared to pay for the presence of a police foot patrol, especially during the hours of darkness. In the UK hospitals have also become prepared to pay for foot patrol; the Headquarters of Devon and Cornwall Constabulary itself employs private security to guard the grounds and check the bona fides of visitors. In the UK at least, the growth of private policing has accompanied the tightening of financial reins on the police and a concomitant redefinition of the core tasks of policing, or what the public purse must pay for. The retreat of police from foot patrol, the privatisation of public space and the increasing insecurity of public life are interpretations placed upon the growth of private policing.

Arguments abound as to the best balance of foot and car patrol and targeted patrol. Patrol is meant to do so many things that it is hard to see how it can deliver on all of them, yet it is equally unlikely that any replacement for it will be found. It is meant to bolster police legitimacy, reassure the public that the police are taking their crime prevention role seriously, smooth the integration of the various communities in a locality, provide local intelligence, deter criminals, respond to local crime problems and provide a safe environment. It is important to be seen to be doing this, perhaps as important as it is to be doing it behind the scenes.

Community relations

The preventive aspects of patrol extend beyond crime prevention into larger issues, concerned with protecting the role of the police as an arm of the state. When the relationship of the police with the community it polices breaks down, serious problems result. Lord Scarman (1981), reporting on the Brixton Riots, found that the way the police had been policing the area had contributed to local perception of the police as heavy handed and racially discriminatory. He also discovered that the police were either unaware of this effect or considered it unimportant. The state of non-communication and hostility between residents and police led to the police failure to recognise a potentially inflammatory situation and to anticipate the reaction of residents. One of the lessons he drew from this was the need for the police to break down barriers between themselves and those they police; to identify local concerns and to accept that effective policing of a locality can only be achieved through dialogue with those policed.

The golden age of policing in the UK, in which law-abiding citizens and their friendly local bobby united to exert a strong moral consensus in the community, is a comfortable myth. However, it is true that the introduction of patrol cars was initially accompanied by the widescale withdrawal of officers from foot patrol. Commentators have linked this withdrawal with a decline in police legitimacy, for patrol cars were introduced during the 1960s, a decade of rapid social and economic change and many types of social unrest. They argue that student demonstrations and widescale industrial picketing could not have occurred had the protagonists respected the right of the police to tell them to disperse; the police were not respected because they had lost their everyday contact with the public.

On a wider West European scale the 1960s and 1970s were the decades in which the post-war generations came of age. Physical and economic structures began to recover from the legacies of the war; technological innovations in manufacturing, telecommunications and mass transport spread rapidly and economic migration became a serious issue. The communities the police were called upon to police became more mobile and less homogenous; and their task more complex. In Dutch cities Eurasian refugees, from newly independent Indonesia, from the Moluccas and from Surinam, formed communities. Emigrants from North Africa settled in France, Spain and Italy. Italy also experienced large-scale internal migration from South to North. Germany invited Turks and Yugoslavs to become 'guest workers', but denied them citizenship. In the UK, communities formed from those who had emigrated from the Indian sub-continent and the West Indies, as had already happened with migrants from Ireland. The migrants brought not only new languages, traditions and values but also different experiences and expectations of policing. Simultaneously, complex forms of youth culture challenged prevailing assumptions about the moral consensus that characterised European societies. All this made new demands for sensitivity on the police (Clarke, 1987).

In the UK, John Alderson, then Chief Constable of Devon and Cornwall Constabulary introduced community policing in the late 1970s. It was not taken up immediately by other forces, but spread during the 1980s, partly as a result of the Scarman Report. It is not unique to the UK; nor does it take any one form. In Germany, for example, officers may not necessarily be foot policing but use their cars to call in on a number of different 'tea stops' to talk to people, show their face and get to know their area and spot what is going on.

The public in any particular locality may be differentiated in a number of ways, such as age, ethnicity, employment status, occupation, length of residence or type of housing occupied. Their expectations and experience of treatment by the police will vary also. Generally, it tends to be young people, members of ethnic minorities and 'police property' (Reiner, 1985) who feel the sharp end of police patrols. They are the individuals who will tend to be asked to account for their presence, explain their movements, and so on. Clearly, those who both live and work in an area are more likely to see the local patrolling officer, especially those working in premises open to the public. The owners of commercial premises may have a complex attitude towards officers. Where the constabulary is involved in the petty corruption of expecting a free cup of tea, a free burger, a free meal or whatever the commercial premises may provide, the owner may or may not see the provision of the service as fair compensation for keeping crime out of their premises and keeping a good name with the police. Where the police are seen as inefficient this petty corruption will be resented.

Apart from generally being seen to be about, patrol and community officers are most likely to come into contact with the local population when a report of petty crime, such as a burglary, has been made. This may simply be because insurance companies require verification of the loss but equally may involve the officer in being more proactive by giving crime prevention advice or in encouraging the establishment of local crime prevention schemes. Community officers may also be involved in visiting local schools to raise crime awareness and promote safe behaviour, or in attending tenants' meetings on housing estates. This kind of low profile work has little kudos or excitement attached to it and perhaps explains its lack of status amongst police officers themselves. One of the persistent problems in community relations policing is that its effectiveness is shown by a lack of anything happening rather than the reverse. Thus those who seek advancement will look to transfer to another branch of policing. Community policing initiatives as a result tend to be staffed by those either at the beginning, or at the end, of their career.

Control room and police station

For most citizens this is the invisible face of policing. The telephone is increasingly the way to contact the police (Punch & Naylor, 1973), and visits to the police station are rare. Verification of driving documents or residence permits are the most frequent reasons for visiting the reception counter of the local 'nick'. Over recent years some attention has been paid to making the atmosphere more friendly and less intimidating, as police services have come to recognise the needs of victims of crime. Nevertheless, the older stations in the major cities of Europe are still unpleasant places. The cell block is not familiar to most people, but the reader can rest assured that there is little variation in the spartan appearance of such places throughout Europe. However, a change is taking place as police services have become more conscious of the rights of the accused, as well as the victim.

The purpose of control rooms is to take decisions about the allocation of police officers in response to calls for assistance or to more general emergencies. In the previous chapter they were described and discussed in detail. There are always more calls coming into police control rooms than there are officers available to answer them. With regard to patrol, the importance of the control room is that it inevitably intervenes to determine what a particular officer is doing, replacing the task given by the patrol officer's shift inspector or immediate superior. Traditionally, an area was policed by a team working to the plan of their supervising officer, but the control room makes this difficult. It also means that preventive patrol is difficult to maintain.

Another important officer is the person in charge of cell provision in a station, called a custody officer in the UK. Increasingly these are judicial officers, even if they are not recognised as such. They take the decisions about whether to hold prisoners or let them free. They decide when a detective can have access to a prisoner for interview and they must keep a log of the interviews taken with a prisoner. The right to sleep and regular meal breaks is becoming more uniform across the European Union, in order that prisoners cannot be interrogated continually over 48 hours, leading to confessions due to sleep deprivation, rather than guilt.

The decisions of the custody officer influence how an officer proceeds during an incident. The custody officer will make clear to the constable what he or she thinks is trivial or important, and thus the patrol officer knows the consequences of bringing a particular prisoner back to the station. The relationship with the custody officer will also determine whether the officer gets burdened with paperwork. In turn this can lead to a summons from a superior to account for time-wasting. In effect, the custody officer has considerable influence on the way in which individual police constables exercise their powers of discretion, arrest, detention and even on whether charges are brought. Both the custody officer and the control room are taking decisions that affect the performance of individual police constables, thereby diminishing the overall responsibility of the shift inspector. The result is that the planned policing of a particular community is increasingly difficult to ensure.

Throughout Europe traditional police notions of hierarchy are being challenged, as a result of technological and legal changes. Rank structures are being altered as a consequence. Police roles can be separated into three: - constable, supervisor and manager. Each of these requires quite different skills, and direct entry to management roles or, at the very least, fast-tracking, is creating a demand for an officer class of a very different sort from that which traditionally existed throughout Continental Europe. Germany solved the problem by eliminating all non-commissioned officer ranks, so everyone is now an officer. The UK abolished three of its nine ranks, where an excess of functional duplication existed. Other countries are in the process of flattening the hierarchy along similar lines. Gendarmeries are likely to be the slowest to complete this process, because their rank structures parallel those of the military of their country.

Practical Issues In Crowd Management

Crowd management is the second most visible face of policing. There have been quite diverse approaches to this area of policing, for which there are many sources. The expectations, on both sides, of what each can expect from the other, affect not only the equipment brought but also the degree and form of forward planning. If uniformity is developing, it is in the appreciation that crowds differ and that there may be more effective ways of proceeding than with instantaneous all-out force.

Whilst the police become more sophisticated in the analysis of crowds, crowd behaviour itself is changing. The policing of crowds and demonstrations regularly provides visual images on the TV news. Its visibility and high news value enable a large proportion of the population to experience this policing vicariously and to form judgements about what has happened. Two issues arise from this: - one is the degree to which violence seen in the media is copied; the other, the degree to which police actions are interpreted negatively, politicising the general public and undermining police and state legitimacy. Whether these are eventually seen as bad things in themselves depends upon one's political standpoint and role, as a police officer or crowd member; as a representative of government or the disenfranchised.

The vicious response to the demonstrators of the Sorbonne in 1968 mobilised the Paris working class, led to *les événements* and to the almost complete collapse of the French state. A similar reaction by the police to students in Prague, in 1968, led to the Prague Spring and an almost total demolition of Communism in Czechoslovakia. In fact, the paranoia it caused Brezhnev and his associates may well have led to the final collapse of Communism, as a consequence of their refusal to countenance any further moves towards economic reform. The events at Burntollet Bridge, also in the late 1960s, led to the demolition of Protestant supremacy in Northern Ireland, the collapse of the Royal Ulster Constabulary and the introduction of the Army to a policing role in the UK, probably for the first time since the early 19th century, although the Army was used in pre-partition Ireland until its independence in 1922.

Changes in police doctrine in the policing of crowds tend to happen as a direct consequence of perceived mishandling. The British learnt their first lesson at Peterloo Fields outside Manchester in 1819. A crowd of demonstrators was met by the county militia and there were several deaths. It was this sort of confrontation that is said to have lead to the birth of the New Police and to the adoption of non-lethal response to crowds and demonstrations. In fact, violence between police and crowds continued through the 19th century and, occasionally, this century. What has distinguished the British police is their determination to avoid violence and their movement towards an attitude of flexible response in the 1970s and 1980s. Until about 1974, the doctrine was 'winning by appearing to lose', a quotation taken from Sir Robert Mark, Commissioner for the Metropolitan Police, at the beginning of the 1970s. The argument he makes is that it is important in each incident that the police win public confidence by appearing to take casualties. The image that people should take away from a demonstration is that of demonstrators getting out of control and injuring the police or, better still, a police horse, rather than an image of the police getting out of control and injuring the demonstrators.

The British approach today is firstly to take into account what the police call 'tension indicators' behind the events leading up to a particular crowd event, be it the Notting Hill Carnival or a demonstration. These tension indicators include reports from the streets of the amount of hostility being shown to officers on routine work, any major incidents with members of particular communities that have occurred and intelligence reports. On the basis of these, the local commander decides what sort of manpower should be available. Such decisions would include whether to provide a few uniformed police to march with the crowd, or be visible in the crowd (depending on the nature of the crowd); whether to have any police in reserve; whether to have a lot of police available; whether to have discussions with the organisers as to what sort of presence might be appropriate or, where a march is concerned, whether the route needs be changed. Generally, each incident is treated on its merits. The appropriate level of policing is decided in terms of numbers and technology available, as well as the sort of uniform to be worn. There is a choice between the traditional British helmet, the flat cap or the space-helmet and fire proof clothing of the full riot squad. Until recently, water cannons and CS gas would not have been considered sensible things to use, but individual constabularies have now equipped individual constables with CS gas sprays. This may lead to incidents in crowd confrontations in the not too distant future.

The Dutch could be said to have learnt this lesson bitterly in the 1970s. At that point, they retreated from technological responses, such as water cannon and tear gas, to an attempt to create a more friendly relationship with Dutch youth and particularly demonstrators in Amsterdam. Outside the main police compound in the Hague is a battered armoured car that is passed by every unit at the start of every patrol. It is there as a grim reminder of what can happen if things get out of control, and that even armoured cars can be broken. This led to the major police reform completed in the early 1990s, in which any remnants of paramilitarism were removed, with the merging of the state police with the municipal police into 25 regional organisations.

The French police see crowds as dangerous. A march or a demonstration is an occasion for violence and must be tightly policed. In this, they are in agreement with the Italians, the Spanish and the Greeks. The Scandinavians and the British would react completely differently. A crowd is to be seen as a group of people to be got from point A to point B safely, and are only to be dealt with in a different way if intelligence provides a reasonable expectation that violence may occur.

At the time of the 1981 riots in Toxteth, Brixton and Southall in England, a couple of articles gave a very good overview of the various ideological attitudes to public disorder. Conservatives believe that institutions are perfect and should be used, thus there is no need to resort to violence. If violence occurs it is because agitators have encouraged it; or because the media have put the idea into people's heads; it is being done for gain; it is being done for entertainment, or it represents some form of mass psychosis. The correct response to this form of violence is either to arrest the agitators, introduce controls on the media, increase the penalties for theft and give people a proper sense of moral values, or arrest the ill for treatment (sending in the social workers). Revolutionaries argue that mass violence is an inevitable sign of a downfall of capitalism and will not disappear until capitalism has fallen. They may or may not be right, but one cannot afford to wait. Liberals, however, believe that institutions are not perfect and that violence is a sign that some response is required. In post-industrial society, it means that wealth should be passed to the protesting community and that institutions should be improved for that community. Lord Scarman (1981) took a liberal view and the results seem to have been extremely positive. The police doctrine of legitimacy has been redefined and, since the end of the Poll Tax, relationships between police and public in England and Wales have improved. The Dutch took a similar decision. The Germans still appear to be tending to blame everything on foreigners and the southern Europeans are keeping their gendarmeries.

It is important to remember that crowd management does not simply consist of dealing with marches, demonstrations, industrial relation disputes and other areas where politically related disorder may occur. There are also football matches and other sports events and open air entertainment to be considered. Similarly, visits by the famous such as the Pope, the football team that has won the cup or a major rock band need policing. The problem of getting the population home when drunk is also a policing problem. A Lancashire policemen estimated that, on a Saturday night at 3.00am, when the pubs and clubs closed, there were 300,000 people to be got from Blackpool to their homes all over the north west. In the late 1980s and early 1990s, there was a period when confrontation with the police was seen as the best way to end a night's entertainment. Every major city has a road of pubs or clubs where such confrontation would take place. These are not the so-called 'no go' areas, characterised by drug dealing, car theft, joy riding and relative deprivation.

The problem for the police at many of these gatherings is facilitating the dispersal of a crowd without danger or confrontation. Since 1983 the Home Office, under its 'value for money' approach, has pressed for the costs of policing public events to be passed to the organiser, especially where the event is a commercial one such as a football match. The costs involved have forced organisers to re-engage stewards, as was the case before the start of football hooliganism in the late 1960s.

Police reponses to public order issues

Whilst some countries have interpreted public disorder as a signal that fundamental change is needed in the organisation of policing, others have treated it as indicating the need for fine-tuning within the existing system, possibly by a shift in policing doctrine or procedure. Others have made no changes, apparently regarding it as requiring more, rather than different, policing. In such countries there is one important difference - the use of a third force especially for riot control. This avoids one of the major problems of using the 'normal' police in policing disorder, the risk that the public will associate the police with the use of force against themselves.

In the UK the policing tradition is very different from policing elsewhere. In 1972, the watershed of the old system was reached at Saltley Coke Depot in Birmingham.

The National Union of Mine Workers and the Trades Council of Birmingham managed to muster 15,000 demonstrators to prevent the passage of coke out of the depot. The police balanced the right to free passage against the likelihood of disorder, if that right continued to be asserted, and decided to close the gates, to prevent disorder and protect the Queen's Peace. In fact they did not have much choice. The West Midlands Constabulary could only call on surplus constables from neighbouring constabularies. There was no national system of providing assistance from one constabulary to another.

This was only instituted with the setting up of the National Reporting Centre during the Miners' Strike of 1984-85, when the 'defeat' of Saltley was replaced by the 'victory' of Orgreave. For the first time in the UK there was a system to organise the delivery of considerable numbers of police constables, from a large number of constabulary areas, to wherever was identified as likely to be subject to mass picketing. For the first time since the General Strike the majority of police officers in the country experienced a prolonged period of operating under discipline, as units rather than individuals; responsible to their immediate senior, be that a sergeant or inspector, rather than to the law in general.

The old system of crowd management was already obsolete before the Miners' Strike. In April 1980, in St Pauls in Bristol, the Avon and Somerset police took a decision to simply throw a cordon around the area and let trouble burn itself out. Similar decisions were taken in Toxteth, Brixton and Southall during 1981 to prevent the crowd from spilling out of the area in which it was rioting. The damage to property resulting from these decisions was unacceptable to the new Thatcher government and general provision of shields, batons, fireproof boots and special helmets with visors was made. Suddenly, UK police officers looked very much like their Continental counterparts. The novels of Sjöwall and Wahloo chronicle a similar process in Sweden during the 1970s.

The need to deploy larger numbers of police personnel led to a completely new police tactical doctrine in the UK. The size of the crowd prepared to indulge in violence and the level of technology its members were prepared to use had changed completely. The 'Gold, Silver, Bronze' system of command was introduced after the Miners' Strike and worked to good effect. 'Gold' designates the officer in charge of the event who should stay in the control room and be responsible purely for overall strategy and deployment; 'Silver' is in charge of tactics for a particular group of police units, usually police transit vans with a number of individuals in each, and may also be in the control room or on the spot; and 'Bronze' is the commander on the spot. The system can change as an incident develops and a commander who was originally Gold can be superseded by a more senior officer as larger numbers of units are required. The system is not only used for crowd management, but for any major incident and is operated by the Ambulance and Fire services as well.

The change in the nature of the crowd that began in the late 1960s made it difficult for the police in the UK to predict whether there was likely to be disorder or not. This in turn led to the creation of the Police Support Units (PSU) that work as a group. During disorder such groups spend a lot of time sitting in a van, waiting to be used, which creates the same sort of 'van mentality' from which the Gendarmerie and CRS suffer. Their time waiting is spent being half-bored, half encouraging each other; and when they are released they tend to assume that this is in order to react violently. Thus they often over-react. In this sense police services are becoming uniform across Europe, although once the British doctrine was that of keeping a police line close to the crowd. The intention was that this closeness would enable police officers and demonstrators to perceive each other as individual human beings, thereby making the outbreak of violence less likely. The tactic of throwing stones from behind by provocateurs led to the abandonment of this tactic, at least in some demonstrations. The British police began to learn riot control from the Hong Kong police where the approach to a crowd is to keep it beyond stone throwing distance and to use whatever non-lethal technology may be of assistance in so doing.

UK police early recognised the need to distinguish a number of groups within a crowd and that, if force was to be used, it had to be used against the right targets. To this extent, the UK doctrine of 'minimum force' survives. The professional demonstrators had to be singled out from the mass of the crowd without provoking that mass to violence. This led to the creation of 'snatch squads', tasked with making brief forays into the crowd to remove the more active rioters while avoiding confrontation with more passive spectators. This is not a lesson that appears to have been learnt across the continent as a whole. The problems of the UK occurred in the 1980s, when it was possible to learn from the failures of crowd management across Western Europe in the 1960s. These led to the terrorism of the 1970s and their legacy has been increasing difficulties for police organisations dealing with the semi-professional demonstrating communities in the major cities of Europe.

The Dutch are the first Continental police organisation to reorganise in response to this problem. Unlike the British, who faced a series of confrontations in industrial relations, their problem related to a revolt of youth based primarily in Amsterdam. As outlined above, after a period of violent confrontations the Dutch introduced major change in both the style and organisation of their policing. The Dutch started off with water cannons, tear gas, special armoured vehicles, visors and shields, and fought it out during the later 1970s and early 1980s. They have, ironically, now chosen complete re-organisation according to what they perceive to be the traditional county-based English style of policing. In doing this they disbanded the state police and de-centralised policing into 25 individual constabulary areas, with a 26th left at national level to provide training, uniforms' intelligence and other appropriate functions. They also introduced a policy of bringing women and ethnic minorities into the police service so that the police service is more representative and better understands the nature of the community it polices. There is a parallel with the Danish free city of Christiania, for the Danes decided to accept Christiania as a no-go area in the name of a 'social experiment'. The UK has not had the same sort of lifestyle confrontation between youth and police in urban areas. The closest it has come is the confrontations with the New Age Travellers at their annual festival at Stonehenge and the diversification of this protest movement into the anti-motorway and by-pass protest movement. Whereas the Dutch and the Danes felt they were taking on the whole of the younger generation, the British have been able to console themselves with the thought that they were only taking on a part.

The French seem not to have changed at all. The Police Nationale and Gendarmerie are still in place. The Police Nationale has a third force or riot police, the CRS, and in a demonstration in Paris, the Gendarmerie and Police Nationale will be responsible for different sectors of the route, with the CRS either in reserve or in place around the actual target of a march. The French police do not seem to be in the least bit concerned about whether or not to use violence. The Gendarmerie frequently do, even against nurses, the CRS always do when they are deployed, and the Police Nationale try to preserve restraint. It may be that the French public can distinguish between the organisations and how they feel about each one. Even the question of civilianising the Gendarmerie seems to be of low priority. However, this is not to say that planning does not take place. One study tour visited a French control room that was primarily concerned with coordinating the efforts of the national police, the Gendarmerie and the CRS to deal with a particular march. At the time the Lycée students were protesting about educational reforms. The difference was that each area was to be the responsibility of a particular unit and the behaviour of the individual officers responsible for a particular area was a matter for their local commander, not to be considered in the light of a total strategy laid down somewhere else.

The difference in approach of the Gendarmerie and the Police Nationale for the areas in which each are responsible can be quite dramatic. The Gendarmerie has a reputation for violence and is extremely easy to provoke. They probably have a worse reputation than the CRS. If the CRS is involved and is called out, the demonstrators seem to have the attitude that this is serious and one must either choose to fight or get out of the way. The CRS will scare off the non-professional demonstrator. The problem with the Gendarmerie is that it can be provoked by the professional demonstrator into violence against the non-professional demonstrator. This is the legacy of the tactics of the late 1960s associated with Cohn-Bendit and known as *contestation*. Students of Herbert Marcuse believed that it was necessary to rip the mask of repressive tolerance off the face of the state and reveal the violence hidden beneath. This was to be done by provoking the security forces into violence against peaceful middle class demonstrators who were usually protesting against the war in Vietnam.

The German response differs from that of the French. The Germans had to respond to a major problem with terrorism. As a result, a large amount of money was invested in the police during the late 1970s and early 1980s. They believe in information technology and the use of databases. The normal Land police are available for small marches and crowds. The Bundesgrenzschutz (BGS) are seen as a disciplined reserve that can be called in where violence is expected and the students in police training colleges are the final reserve when a mass of police is required for dealing with a particularly unruly crowd. The cadets at police college are under discipline and young and therefore are prone to obey orders. Across southern Europe the pattern is similar. The paramilitary police are used as a reserve where violence is expected and tend to obtain the violence expected fairly easily. Most countries, as well as having their normal paramilitary police, have a specialist riot squad such as the CRS whose job it is to protect particular buildings or to clear the crowd.

In Spain the situation is extremely complex. The fall of the post-Franco regime, and its replacement by democracy, has led to decentralisation of some government powers to the Autonomous Communities, of which the most notable are the Basques and the Catalans. When the Autonomous Communities were created they were given the right to create their own police forces. The Basques responded immediately in 1985, and the Catalans more recently. The central problem is the continuing existence, unreformed, of the Guardia Civil, a paramilitary force with a controversial past under the Franco regime, as has the Policia Nacional. Over the period from 1985 to 1986 policing in the three Basque provinces has been taken over by the Ertzaintza, step by step.

The Ertzaintza began with foot patrol in the rural areas, moved up to a mixture of car and foot patrol as they took over responsibility in the smaller towns, and then finally replaced the municipal police in the major cities. The Guardia Civil retreated to a purely military role and are only visible in a few barracks in the major cities. They also maintain responsibility for the borders for political reasons – to give the Basques responsibility for the borders with France would be taking a step too far towards statehood.

The Catalans have not gone quite so far with their autonomous police and have allowed the Police Nationale and Guardia Civil to retain more of the expensive functions of policing, such as maintaining forensic science laboratories and technical equipment. The basic principle underlying the initiative is to remove the remnants of Franco's regime from the streets and improve the legitimacy of the uniformed police. At least two other Autonomous Communities in Spain are studying the Basque and Catalan experience with a view to introducing their own local police services. It is worth noting, however, that when the Basques set up their new police and began the process of removing the Guardia Civil they made sure that they had a riot squad with armoured vehicles in reserve and a paramilitary capability. This still gives them the capacity for flexible response and, despite their increase in legitimacy, they have needed it, particularly in San Sebastian during the summer.

The Danes, as noted earlier, went along with the Dutch. The Italians have begun to change their legal system but have not satisfactorily re-organised their police, nor have the French. A possible reason for this is that they were already geared up to dealing with violence in all its variety, and therefore feel that they have nothing to learn but more to teach the other European states.

There are three possible ways of dealing with a crowd that has become unruly, assuming that the crowd is not to be allowed to pass in as orderly a fashion as possible. The crowd can be contained, cleared or crushed. Containment is simply the throwing around the crowd of a cordon; that is the task carried out by a large body of police officers such as the German cadets. Clearing is a situation in which the crowd is to be moved from the streets and this usually involves the use of non-lethal weapons such as batons, water cannons and CS gas. On occasion, police commanders or political superiors decide that a particular group needs to be taught a lesson; then the crowd is deliberately trapped and severely beaten, gassed, or whatever form of technology is available can be used against it. This latter approach does not have a history of success. It tends to produce a long-term problem with the community concerned and expectations of future violence.

In countries with competing police services like Belgium and France, the opportunities for disaster to occur due to disagreements or conflicts of responsibility are high. The Heysel Stadium disaster is a case in point. The problem occurred because the area separating the Italian and Liverpool fans also marked the border of responsibility between the Gendarmerie and the municipal police. Thus when a confrontation took place, it occurred on the line of demarcation, and this inhibited the response.

Differences in crowd behaviour

The prevailing image of crowd management in the UK is that of a large column of people walking down a road accompanied by one or two police officers looking slightly bored. The good humoured nature of the English crowd has long been a source of envy amongst foreign police officers. There is a well established debate as to whether crowds in the UK are good humoured because of the low level of intervention by the police, or whether the police can maintain a low level of intervention because of the good humoured nature of the crowd.

There are revisionist historians who would say that the single issue of political demonstration may have a peaceful history in the UK, but that this is not true of industrial relations. Throughout the 19th and 20th centuries there have been outbreaks of violent confrontation at picket lines throughout the UK. These have involved pushing and shoving, rather than the throwing of stones or Molotov cocktails.

The situation first changed with the appearance of the National Front in 1967, which began marching to provoke a violent reaction from left wingers and members of ethnic minorities. It successfully caused the police to interpose themselves between National Front marchers and counter-demonstrators in the name of the right to free speech. It was not until the 1980s that the police finally obtained the right to determine the route of a march well in advance of the march taking place.

The right to determine the route of a march and indeed the ability to hold the organisers of a march financially responsible for damage have long been in place in France. Here the television image has been quite different, particularly in 1968 when large numbers of students and workers poured onto the streets. The draconian legal structure within which demonstrations and marches take place in France seems to have little effect on the incidence of confrontation and violence during these events. Indeed it has been said that the French like to have a revolution at least once in their lifetime. But the events of Paris in 1968 were paralleled in Italy, Germany, Christiania in Copenhagen, Amsterdam and, to a lesser degree the UK, in the anti-Vietnam march to the American Embassy of Grosvenor Square in 1968.

Whether the National Front marches of the 1970s led to a decline in police legitimacy in the areas with concentrations of immigrants, and thus to a preparedness on the part of these individuals to use violence, is a moot point. One might ask whether, in the aftermath of the Miners' Strike, removing policing from most urban areas to the places where picketing was anticipated, created an atmosphere of lawlessness, or whether the nature of the confrontations, as seen on the television, created a preparedness to use violence for entertainment in a distorted copying of the show on the news.

The peaceful nature of the British crowd may not simply have been to do with the absence of a culture of violence, but may also have been due to the role of the steward. Until the 1960s both football matches and demonstrations were extremely well stewarded. Most of the people concerned were volunteers, they were part of the crowd, and they understood how to communicate with the crowd in a non-antagonistic way. Stewards seemed to disappear in the middle to late 1960s, both on demonstrations and at football matches. Their disappearance at demonstrations may have been associated with the move from the old Communist Party to a Trotskyite approach. The Communist Party always placed a high premium on discipline and the avoidance of unnecessary confrontation. The new line of the Fourth International after 1967–68, the appearance of Maoism as a challenge to traditional communism, as well as the resurgence of anarchism, meant that leadership roles within the crowd were being performed by people from different organisations whose interests were not those of the traditional role of the steward. The crowd was thus no longer organised by individuals who accepted some responsibility for keeping it in order.

It is interesting that a movement towards uniformity, on the part of the crowds themselves, can be observed. The totally peaceful British crowd is a thing of the past; the structured crowd with a peaceful majority and a confrontational minority is characteristic of crowds right across the European Union, even when these are football crowds rather than political crowds.

This raises a series of interesting questions for future researchers— is the population of the UK becoming more Europeanised and learning European habits of protest, to which the police are responding? Is the separateness of the UK thereby increasingly a myth? Or is this a normal consequence of the police becoming more of a national organisation? Does the important customer become the state as a consequence, and is the state incapable of responding to peaceful legitimate political demands? Do the years of one party government from 1979 to 1997 parallel the similar problems of the Gaulliste era and of the Christian Democrats in Italy? In other words, is this a problem of politicians rather than of the police ? Consequent on that, do we want a police service to be so organised that politicians can buy indefinite relief from the unpopular consequences of their policies, or organised so that only short term political relief can be bought?

In an era of globalisation, when governments believe there is little they can do in the way of governing, the pressure is for an evermore efficient police service. The French model may be attractive, with three different organisations who can respond to public disorder with increasing levels of force. It has the advantage that the people who serve out the worst levels of force are not the people who patrol the streets on a daily basis. It is a very expensive option. A return to the politics of democratic consent is not only more pleasant for the citizenry but a great deal cheaper in the long run.

Conclusion

Traditionally policing was identical to foot patrol. The advent of new technologies has dramatically changed what police officers do and, thus, what policing is. Foot patrol was conceived of as preventive, both of crime and of public disorder. Since policing, in the sense of what police officers do, is now primarily an emergency response system, police services and publics across Europe have problems in dealing with this new state of affairs. Philosophies of policing are now at odds with reality. Police organisations are struggling to reorganise in recognition of changed circumstances. The priorities of the public, the state, local government and the business community are in conflict and the police have new competitors from the private sector offering these customers a choice of services.

Technological innovation is not alone in its impact on policing. The nature of social and political conflict has also changed and with it the way individuals behave when in crowds. This also makes demands on police management and leadership structures. There are at least five different organisational models of crowd management currently in operation. The way in which crowd control is apportioned is the significant variable, reflecting differing attitudes to public disorder, and to the way in which the legitimacy of the police should be maintained:

- the England and Wales model, based on the notion of the competent flexible constable who is expected one day to be part of a disciplined fighting machine, the next to be an effective community police officer;
- the French model, in which the Police Nationale, Gendarmerie and the CRS all perform different roles at different times in relation to crowd patrol;
- the Northern Ireland model, in which the police use the army as a reservoir of extra manpower for keeping two communities apart, and for dealing with demands on personnel that are simply impossible to cope with;
- the German model where the third force are the officers in training;
- the Dutch model, which is to make the police more representative of the community in terms of gender and ethnicity.

These changes raise major questions about police accountability and legitimacy which will be addressed in the next chapter.

5. Police Legitimacy and Accountability

Introduction

An important source of difference between police systems is the degree to which the police are subject to supervision by legal and political authorities. As already noted in Chapter 1, in most of continental Europe a distinction is drawn between the missions of different police services: - there are those which are charged with law enforcement and those which are charged with public order responsibilities. In essence, this separation is one between the investigation of crime and what would be called in the UK uniform patrol work and response. In many continental systems the uniform police are subject to some form of political supervision, either through centrally appointed prefects who are in charge of local government or through elected majors. Criminal investigation is under the supervision of a judge, a procurator/prosecutor/district attorney or a combination of the two. This presents problems for police officers, politicians and lawyers in England, where opposition to a role for the European Court continues. This is the only body, short of a European Ministry of Justice, from which cross-border judicial supervisors could be appointed to oversee Europol, Schengen, UCLAF and the other supranational police bodies to be discussed in Chapter 6.

The interplay between how the police are organised, what they do and how they do it, and most importantly, whom they are seen as doing it for, affects the degree of legitimacy that the police are accorded by those they police. This chapter discusses the traditional UK model of police legitimacy, including a continental European perspective, before analysing its relevance to investigation and crowd management. It then examines European systems of accountability before turning to the new right wing doctrine of accountability to the market. It finishes with a discussion of the exercise of discretion by the uniform police.

Legitimacy

Legitimacy is a key concept in discussing the police. It is related to, but is not the same as, accountability. Whilst means of holding the police accountable for their actions are important, ultimately if the police are not accepted by the public as having the right to perform their role, civil unrest and disorder will follow. If the police are used incautiously and aggressively to counter this, there is a real threat that a challenge to the political order will follow.

The UK model

Robert Reiner (1985), in his book *The Politics of the Police*, suggests eight headings that characterise the traditional British model of police legitimacy. They are:
- bureaucratic organisation, including the concept of professionalism;

- rule of law, including the idea that the police are accountable to the law and the courts;
- minimum force which might be taken to include the idea of a non-armed police;
- non-partisanship which includes the idea of enforcing the law without fear or favour;
- service role;
- preventive policing, including the idea of preventive patrol and the priority of prevention over detection;
- effectiveness, including the idea that the police offer a more effective route to justice than personal settling of scores;
- incorporation of the working class, with the aim of ensuring that the police are part of the population policed, thereby removing a source of antagonism and hostility.

In terms of bureaucratic organisation the essence of British legitimacy comes from a 'bottom-up' perspective in which the individual constable has a high degree of discretion as to how law is enforced. Under the concept of the rule of law, the law cannot be separated from the courts. The constable is responsible to the law for his or her actions and has to decide whether an order from a superior is, or is not, lawful.

Reiner's principles require some reinterpretation in the light of technological and social changes since their publication (Tupman, 1992a). The doctrine of minimum force has been re-interpreted in post-1960s western society. The concept of minimum appropriate force, or of flexible response, is now more commonly used. Conflict and demonstrations are an essential part of contemporary democracy and all police forces are having to learn to distinguish between the aims of demonstrators and the means they use. Increasingly, crowd management is a science. It is difficult for the police to deal with the public effectively and acceptably if the politicians are alienating sections of the public. In the last ten years there has also been quite dramatic change in the areas covered by Reiner's last four headings. The service role, for example, has now been restated as the doctrine of Quality of Service, the Association of Chief Police Officers (ACPO) has become 'customer aware', and is trying to reconcile the demands of various customers: politicians, citizens, victims of crime, detainees awaiting trial, etc. The latest *Statement of Common Purpose and Values* from the Metropolitan Police (1997), now says, with emphasis from the original:

> The purpose of the Metropolitan Police Service is to uphold the law fairly and firmly; to *prevent crime*; to pursue and bring to justice those who break the law; to keep *The Queen's Peace* to protect, help and reassure people in *London*; and to be seen to do all this with integrity, common sense and sound judgement.
>
> We must be *compassionate*, courteous and patient, acting without fear or favour or prejudice to the rights of others. We need to be professional, calm and restrained in the face of violence and apply only that force which is necessary to accomplish our lawful duty.
>
> We must strive to reduce the fears of the public and, so far as we can, to reflect their

priorities in the action we take. We must respond to *well-founded criticism* with a willingness to change.

The reassertion of the service role in the UK is related to preventive policing and police effectiveness. From the 1960s onwards, the UK police force fell, to some extent, into the trap of the doctrine of reactive policing. One of the easiest things to measure in terms of police effectiveness used to be the time it took for a police officer to react to a call for assistance from the public. Coupled with the arrival of radios, cars and control rooms, a number of police forces moved away from preventive policing and the foot patrol to reactive policing, thereby losing a regular, non-conflict based relationship with the community (Clarke, 1987).

The incorporation of the working class has now been modernised to include equal opportunities. Western police forces now seek to incorporate not only the working class, but also women, ethnic minorities and minorities of sexual preference. The UK has not gone so far as to establish quotas, but ACPO has stated that more women and ethnic minorities should be recruited. It has also made it clear that homosexuals have a place within the constabulary and should not suffer discrimination.

The British police learned the need for a good relationship with the public during the 19th century. Modern research has re-stressed that it is the public who report crime, the public who have to be relied on to be witnesses in court and to be prepared to serve on juries to decide the guilt or innocence of accused persons. In many ways, the police cannot successfully carry out their tasks unless the public are prepared to look at them in a positive light. It is in this context that, since the Miners' Strike of 1984-85, police leaders have sought to re-interpret and modernise the doctrine of police legitimacy.

In the aftermath of the ratification of the Treaty of Maastricht, which includes the declaration of police cooperation and Article K on cooperation in the field of Home Affairs and Criminal Justice, all police services are trying to learn good practice from each other and to combine the best ideas whilst maintaining those features that reflect the culture of the country or region in which the police operate. Most European democrats admire the English principles of :

- 'policing by consent', by which is meant the tradition of policing the rules the community concerned wants to have policed. This involves a high exercise of discretion on the part of the individual constable. It also involves close contact between the higher ranks and the local political authorities. At times it can lead to conflict with the judiciary's stress on the rule of law. This principle recognises that without the consent of the general public, crime will not be reported, witnesses will not come forward and evidence will not be given in court;
- 'bottom-up', not 'top-down': this relates to the powers and importance of the constable in the UK and the absence of a direct-entry officer class, although accelerated promotion in the name of efficient management may be wrecking this. Other countries have procedures whereby constables can rise to be officers;
- the unarmed tradition: patrol officers in the UK are unarmed. A percentage of the constabulary is trained to handle firearms, but these are only carried by armed response vehicles and by officers of the Diplomatic Protection Group and others

engaged in VIP protection. In the majority of the European Union, as in the United States, patrol officers normally carry a firearm;

- the myth of the efficiency of Scotland Yard: whether as a result of films, books or actual experience of working together, 'Scotland Yard' is still perceived as having the best detectives, despite the fact that Regional Crime Squads were set up in 1964 and no Chief Constable has had to call in the Yard for special expertise since then. Hidden inside this myth is the idea that British detectives are not susceptible to political interference and are consummate professionals, aware of the ways of criminals and of the problem of gathering evidence rather than information.

Most continental democrats, despite British confidence in the superiority of the UK system in protecting 'liberty', look askance at the absence in the UK of a Ministry of Justice tasked with ensuring the reconciliation of the day-to-day working of the system with absolute principles of Justice enshrined in a written constitution. They also have problems with the similar absence of judicial supervision of the detective branch in England and Wales. 'Non-partisanship' is not considered to be adequately safeguarded, given the UK's adversarial political system. Some continental officers would argue that the involvement of individual police officers in political parties is not harmful in the context of a multi-party, proportional representation system, in which government is always a coalition and consensus and compromise have to be reached. There is thus some disagreement about which systems of political and judicial accountability best preserve the legitimacy of the police and criminal justice system.

Although there are elements of myth in what is seen as characterising the best of the British policing model, which in some ways has been overtaken by events, there is still agreement on its goals: the gaining and keeping of public support; making the police truly representative of the population policed, and the impartial maintenance of the interests of justice and fairness rather than political favour. There is less agreement on the effectiveness of the structures that are meant to ensure the attainment of these goals. Other European countries have arrived at different organisational means, within different kinds of criminal justice systems, to achieve these goals.

Legitimacy and public opinion

Legitimacy is a central concept for policing because it is impossible for the police to investigate every crime or incident of public disorder. The police depend upon the cooperation of the rest of the public. In the case of public disorder, they depend upon a large proportion of the crowd to recognise their right to stop disorder, to then take the decision to stop participating in the disorder and either leave the scene or become spectators rather than participants. In the case of crime, the police depend upon citizens to report crime, usually via the telephone, although occasionally by arriving at a police station. They also depend on the citizen to be prepared to provide evidence and to undergo cross examination, either by the procurator in inquisitorial systems or, under the English adversarial criminal justice system, by barristers for the defence.

How the citizens view the police is thus an important variable in the criminal justice system. It is also an important variable in the success or failure of the political system. The way in which the police deal with crowds, especially those which are engaged in

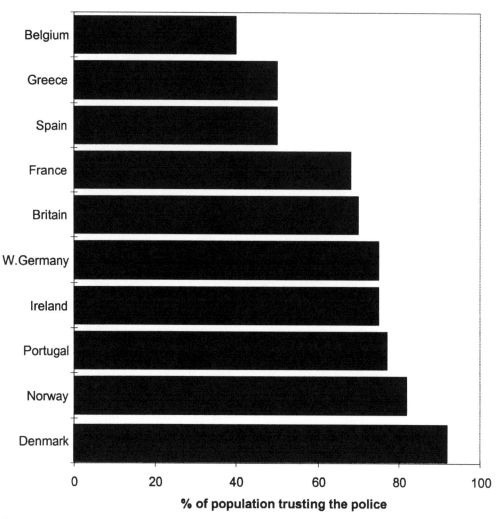

Figure I .Trust in the Police (Source: Politikan)

political activity, has a major impact on the legitimacy of the political system. A police service that avoids violent confrontation and places a high premium on the safe passage of the citizen will have more legitimacy than a police service that engages in a competition of violence. Where politicians use police force in order to ignore legitimate public demands, both the political system and the police suffer. A counter argument that is sometimes used by politicians and senior police officers is that they are attempting to police a violent culture. It is very difficult to disentangle whether the violence is a result of police action, or the raison d'être for police action. Legitimacy also seems to be sensitive to the public perception of what constitutes justifiable police action. The definition encompasses efficiency and discretion. A 'good' police service that is not efficient in catching criminals will lose the confidence of the public, as will a police service that is perceived as petty, and always enforcing minor rules.

Figure I shows the percentage of people who said they trusted their police force. According to this, the police have high legitimacy in Scandinavia. The difference between Spain and Portugal presumably has come about as a result of the civilianisation of the police in Portugal, while the low levels of confidence accorded to the police in Spain may be explained by high levels of unpopularity in both the Basque Country and Catalonia. There is great similarity between the figures for Britain and France, which does not accord with popular belief in England about the comparative trustworthiness of the two, although it does tend to support the view that many of the factors giving the police legitimacy, summarised by Reiner, no longer represent the truth of policing on the ground, although they may well have held true in the past.

Legitimacy and the investigative function

Just as reaction time has become a major indicator against which the uniformed police are measured, European detectives also have to demonstrate effectiveness and efficiency. Despite everything that was discussed in Chapter 2 about the different roles performed under the general heading of policing, the media tend to focus on a single, easily understood indicator: the clear-up rate (percentage of crimes for which an offender is identified by the police). Table XVI was presented on a Swedish television programme on 10 July 1996 (Sigma, 1996).

Like much of the statistical information presented elsewhere in this book, data are not available for all European countries, but in this case, only Italy and the UK are missing. It should not be surprising that Sweden occupies such a low place in the league table, since the table was broadcast by Swedish news. The figure is comparable to the clear-up rate for the Metropolitan Police if the 'dark figure' of crime (unreported) is included (Hough & Mayhew, 1983). Victim surveys around the world demonstrate that on average, two crimes go unreported for every crime committed. The implications for police legitimacy are profound. If only 10-20 per cent of crime is solved, there are many victims of crime who will not consider that the police are doing their job. A

Country	% crime solved 1993
Japan	72.6
Ireland	29.1
Norway	22.09
Luxembourg	19.24
Greece	17.6
Austria	17.3
Canada	16.92
USA	13.1
Germany	12.5
France	12.22
Portugal	11.1
Spain	10.57
Denmark	10.4
Netherlands	10
Sweden	8
Belgium	7

Table XVI. International Crime Clearup Rates, 1993 (Source: Sigma)

statement by a former Swedish Chief of Police, taken from the source from which Table XVI derives, is apposite:

> A police force with 100 years of experience has fallen apart in no time at all. Nowadays we investigate shoplifting and homicides but neglect the everyday crimes between these two extremes.

Legitimacy and crowd management

This section examines the implications of crowd management for legitimacy. The concept of the 'third force' was originally based on an identified need for an organisation that was neither the police nor the army. The army is an organisation devoted to the use of lethal force. The police in the UK context has long been unarmed and is dedicated to the use of non-lethal force when force is required. A third force, between the two, was conceived of as an organisation that could deliver disciplined non-lethal force using batons, shields and wearing flame-resistant clothes and the like. There are cost implications in having such an organisation. There is also the problem of what to do with it when it is not dealing with disorder. This is one of the reasons for the use of students in police training colleges as a reserve, in countries that have a long period of police training. This is also known as the 'Hong Kong' or 'British Colonial' model.

The argument for a third force, specialising in riot control, is that the normal police need to be protected from the loss of legitimacy that results from violence against the public. It is argued that a third force needs to be disciplined, whereas members of an ordinary patrol force need to be able to exercise their own initiative and judgement. The advantage of discipline is that people obey orders. The disadvantage is that they do not know what to do when they have no orders. Most everyday policing is carried out by individuals acting on their own, or in pairs. Under these circumstances they need to be capable of judging the situation for themselves and taking appropriate action, rather than radioing in for instructions every 30 seconds or calling for assistance at the slightest threat of confrontation. An ordinary patrol constable needs to be good at diffusing conflict, rather than fighting it out.

The high cost of these forces and the fact that they are only required for very short periods of time in any particular 12 months, leads to their use in some sort of policing back-up job. Since they already have little legitimacy, this creates serious problems for them when dealing with the public. It is claimed that for politicians to have such an instrument under their control is dangerous. Instead of dealing with problems that have caused public outrage, they can try to use violence to make those problems go away. This is not good for the democratic system, as it allows politicians to ignore legitimate public demand. The decisive questions to be answered are whether there is a residual role for a police service with military capabilities, and whether a third force with a riot control role is required by central government. The Germans have a system whereby riot duty is performed by cadets under training, with an occasional role for the Bundesgrenzschutz (BGS), a border police, but one that wears British Army Second World War-style battledress and gaiters, and is based in barracks. The French have the

CRS, a unit under the Police Nationale rather than under the Gendarmerie, so theoretically civilian. The problem with units like the CRS is finding work for them when there are no riots, just as it was difficult to find work for the Gendarmerie outside wartime.

The form conflict takes and the likelihood of it reaching the streets are affected by various factors. The division of society into rural and urban areas has been mentioned, but there are religious and linguistic divisions which also affect the likelihood of serious public disorder. Public disorder is most likely to be serious where two communities are fighting against each other, rather than one group using violence to lobby the state to preserve or alter its way of life or to obtain more resources. All these will affect the form that the policing of public disorder takes, both organisationally and in terms of style.

The need for multiple forces reflects the state of legitimacy of the organisations involved. In general terms, the greater the level of legitimacy, the less there is a need for coercive force to obtain compliance with the state or sub-state institution's wishes. Thus low levels of legitimacy demand high levels of force. In policing, it is not just a matter of measuring legitimacy across the whole of society, but in specific geographical areas and particular ethnic and social groups. For example, the RUC has low levels of legitimacy among Northern Irish Catholics, as does the Guardia Civil among Basques. Both organisations are caught in a vicious circle, because low levels of legitimacy and high levels of social conflict inevitably lead to frequent violent clashes between police and community, which in turn means that legitimacy inevitably stays at a low level. The creation of the Ertzaintza is an attempt to escape this cycle by trying to create a police service that the Basques can call their own. It should thus have high levels of legitimacy, which in turn should mean that it can rely on using low levels of violence. However, it still suffers from the general alienation between police and young people in general, probably because of the conservatism of the Basque National Party.

Accountability

To enjoy legitimacy in a democracy, a police service has to provide what the public want. Given their missions, there is always a danger that the police will argue, in the terms of Rousseau, that they embody the General Will, and are not subject to the Tyranny of the Majority. Therefore there must be a mechanism by which the public communicate their reactions to the police. Most police systems will have a complaints system, under which individual members of the public can complain about the actions of officers.

An accountability system, on the other hand, is a mechanism by which comment can be made on general policy. Most democratic systems accept that such comment is best made by elected representatives of the public, but police actions are also subject to the rule of law, which can only be represented by magistrates, judges and / or prosecutors. Thus the relationship between the police and local government, the police and national government and the police and judicial authorities is also termed 'accountability'. There is room for argument within a democracy about whether, at a particular time, nationally or locally elected representatives are more truly representative of the public in their comments. As accountability is in many ways a power relationship, there is frequently a problem of checks and balances. This is particularly true in periods when a government is attempting to change citizen behaviour, or is strongly resisting demands for change in its own behaviour.

The way in which accountability is catered for varies greatly depending on the type of judicial and political systems. Until 1964 the UK had different models of accountability for rural and urban areas. In the urban areas local politicians dominated the Watch Committees, which set policing priorities as well as influencing promotions and discipline. In the rural areas the judicial authorities predominated through a mixture of elected representatives and magistrates. The Home Office, at national level, was largely a conduit through which some of the national tax revenue was transferred to local authorities for police funding. All this changed with the 1964 Police Act. This replaced Watch Committees with Police Authorities, apparently modelled on the rural system pre-dating 1964, and in effect transferred significant amounts of power away from local government and politics. The new system became known as the Tripartite system. The Chief Constable was responsible for day-to-day policing to both the Home Office nationally and the Police Authority locally.

There was no clear demarcation as to who had power over what. When the Thatcher Government came to power in 1979, with a clear agenda of breaking trade union power, conflict was inevitable. The Police Authorities in the cities were largely Labour councillors and Labour-appointed magistrates. The political conflict which followed culminated in the Miners' Strike of 1984-85. Power effectively passed to the Home Office. This was further strengthened after Home Office Circular 114/83 and its successors 105 and 106/85 caused radical change in the ways forces were staffed, funded and managed. It rapidly emerged, however, that significant power also had been transferred to the Chief Constable and that the subsequent merger of police forces, reducing their number from 120 to 43 in England and Wales and 8 in Scotland, had created a number of powerful independent figures who used special knowledge and expertise as an excuse for ignoring the priorities of local politicians. Their slogan was 'who really represents the community?'. The third element of the Tripartite system, the local police authority, was the loser in the process. The Dutch reform of the early 1990s was very similar in conception to the 1964 Act in the UK, and it will be worth watching to see if the same results take place.

As a result of the recommendations of the Scarman inquiry into the Brixton and other riots of 1980 and 1981, consultative committees were set up under S.106 of the Police and Criminal Evidence Act of 1984. This was an attempt to provide more local contact between police and community (Morgan, 1989). In England and Wales accountability had become little more than a Chief Constable justifying actions after the event to a police authority, or an officer of lesser rank lecturing a 'consultative' committee.

A system with three elements in it also exists in the Netherlands and Belgium. The Dutch call it the 'Triangle'. The Table below is derived from one used in the late 1980s and early 1990s by staff of the Dutch Police Academy at Apeldoorn to explain their system to English-speakers. At the time there were 149 police forces in the Netherlands.

	Task/mission	Municipal Force	State Police
Supervision	Maintaining order	Burgomeister	Ministry of Interior
Supervision	Law enforcement	Public prosecutor	Public prosecutor
Management		Burgomeister	Ministry of Justice
Where?		Towns over 25,000	Rural areas

Table XVII. Dutch Policing before the reform

One of them, the Rijkspolitie, had 14,000 officers, while the other 148 shared 22,000 personnel and varied in size from 41 members to 3,300.

Although apparently complex, the Dutch system was not that different to the system prevailing in England and Wales before the Police Act of 1964, with one important proviso. Instead of there being a constabulary for each county, it is as if all the non-county borough forces, in effect the rural forces, had been amalgamated into a single unit. Indeed, an urban-rural divide in systems of accountability is not unusual in Europe. As noted in Chapter 1, a number of continental countries have a gendarmerie that is partly funded and controlled by the Ministry of Defence and has a wartime function of preventing desertion from the battlefront. In peace time it is responsible for patrolling and investigating crime in rural areas and also frequently acts as a government reserve in times of public disorder, particularly during industrial disputes. The Dutch State Police were, in effect, a civilianised gendarmerie.

Under the Dutch model today it is fairly simple to understand the relationship between local politicians, represented by the Burgomeister, and the judicial authorities, represented by the Procurator. What is interesting is that an individual constable or an individual policing unit can be responsible to one official, the Burgomeister, whilst being responsible for the maintenance of order, and to a quite different official, the Public Prosecutor, for the enforcement of the law. The Chief Constable is responsible for implementing the policies of these two officials in day-to-day policing. In the familiar division of post-Napoleonic police services, the state police deals with the rural areas and the municipal police deals with towns over 10,000. The creation of the triangle of the Chief Procurator, the Chief Constable and the Burgomeister was in itself a simple organisational way of minimizing the conflicts inherent in the overlapping division of power between the Procurator and the Burgomeister. Historically, the Burgomeister was primarily concerned with public order or public tranquility and therefore concerned with preventing violence on the streets and increasing the population's sense of security, but would also have had to respond to demands from his electorate for more resources to deal with specific crimes that made them feel threatened. This might have been an invasion of the Procurator's territory of overall control of crime investigation.

However, the idea of a regular meeting between the three individuals most concerned with crime, violence, safety and security, is a typically Dutch pragmatic solution to what could have become an in-built source of permanent conflict. The three officers will meet at least once a month, and in times of particular problems will negotiate agreed policies. It is worth noting that the Chief Constable also has to negotiate these policies with representatives of the various trade unions that exist within the police service.

As discussed in Chapter 3, a procurator or a judge is involved in the process of investigating crime partly because of their responsibility for ensuring that investigation is carried out in a fair and just fashion, and partly because it is useful to have someone to judge whether information is really evidence that can be used in a court of law to prove guilt or innocence. As employees of the Ministry of Justice, they have a role to protect the human rights of the suspect and balance those against the human rights of the victim. Their decisions frequently have implications for resource allocation. This in turn affects the setting of investigative priorities. In those systems that give them a role in investigation, they will represent the priorities of the Ministry of Justice against those of the Ministry of the Interior, represented by the Burgomeister, Prefect or other official. This provides democratic control through a system of checks and balances. It can still fail, as it may be thought to have done in Belgium during the investigation and detention of a noted paedophile in 1998, because there may be interference from a national level. The careers of not only the Ministers of Justice and the Interior, but also the Prime Minister, were at stake in that case.

When judicial accountability works well, it can lead to changes in policy and practice after judicial review of racial and sexual discrimination in employment, or even, following successful appeals into miscarriages of justice, to the prosecution of the officers concerned. If 'Justice' is taken as the principle to which judicial officers are ultimately responsible, their role is to resist public demands which are against the principles of human rights. Thus judicial authorities can resist knee jerk reactions, moral panics and witch hunts more successfully than political officials. On the other hand, if they are primarily acting as guardians of social justice, their role may be more that of balancing these public demands and the principles of human rights against each other. Clearly this will affect the way in which they relate to the police and the local authorities.

It can be seen, therefore, that because of the different missions of policing a system of police accountability has to provide a role for national government, local government, judicial authorities and police management. European systems differ over:

- whether the judicial authority is a judge or a prosecutor (discussed in Chapter 3);
- whether the local government officer is locally elected (a mayor) or appointed by central government (a prefect);
- whether there is a representative of the local business community (England and Wales);
- whether there is a federal system (Germany, and in a partial sense, Spain);
- whether there are consultative committees for subdivisions within a local government unit.

The French have the most centralised system and the Belgians the most decentralized. The whole of Belgium is divided into municipalities, each of which has its own police force. There is no separate rural area for the Gendarmerie to police, which is why the two organisations compete for work. In France, nothing is possible without consultations with Paris. The Prefect is the local representative of Paris. The juge d'instruction is the only individual within the French system who can claim some independence of action.

In the German model clear divisions of power exist between the Central Government and the Länder. There were ten Länder in the original West German state; on re-unification East Germany added a further six. Despite potential advantages, the Federal model remains unattractive to the majority of states in the European Union.

Accountability to the market: effectiveness and efficiency

Politicians of the new, free-market right argue that accountability to politicians is actually ineffective. The way in which the public will obtain what they want is if the police, like any other service industry, are subject to market forces and competition with private sector organisations.

Upon examination this does not stand up. Police services in urban areas traditionally were accountable more to elected local politicians than were police services in rural areas. Governments traditionally have invested more in man-power in rural areas than the local crime demands justify. Modern reformers trying to maximise efficiency, however defined, want to release rural resources for the increasingly populated urban areas. Moves to promote efficiency go hand-in-hand with pressures for national control, so that resources may be switched from area to area as required. Those seeking efficiency pursue only measurable goals which are dictated by trends in crime, arrest rates and responses to telephone calls. Legitimacy, however is not measurable. Nor is the prevention of crime or the impact of a close relationship between a local police service and a local community. Yet the rural area with low levels of reported crime is perceived by the accountant as not requiring the police resources based within it. This is true of the gendarmeries, the Garda Síochána outside Dublin, and oddly, the Belgian municipal forces rather than the Belgian Gendarmerie.

Other changes affect perceptions of the gendarmerie. For example, the historical importance of the peasantry, particularly in France and Germany, may have produced a perception that a separate force was required for rural areas. But the political importance of the peasantry has declined dramatically over the past 10 to 15 years. This in turn has produced changes in the pattern of support for political parties and caused a re-examination of the costs of maintaining a different system of policing for rural areas. The collapse of communism has also led to a re-examination of the Defence budget and pressure for the removal of policing from the military budget.

Important changes are also taking place in the size of the residential community that is characteristic of a particular country (Smith, 1989). The UK is untypical with 58 per cent of the population living in cities of over 100,000. The German equivalent figure is 34 per cent and France, 33 per cent. A figure of around 30 per cent appears to be the norm, with Portugal at 12 per cent representing the other extreme to Britain. These figures conceal, Smith argues, an overall decline to 10 per cent of the population being involved in agriculture in most of western Europe, as opposed to 2 per cent in Britain. Thus 'rural' areas are no longer characterised by values different to those of the towns. Patterns of politics and crime, in the past, differed strongly between urban and rural areas and thus affected both the style of policing, the nature of the organisation providing the service and the nature of the community being policed. This difference is being gradually erased and policing changes should follow.

A market-based approach leads to the question of identifying the 'customer' of the police service; is it central government, local government or the judicial authorities? The various political traditions of European countries have placed different emphases on the importance of these historically, and do so today. Whilst it is difficult to generalise about countries and their characteristics without falling prey to various stereotypes, it is possible to discuss relevant characteristics of the various administrative systems that may be found.

In the UK the influence of local government has been in decline since 1979 and that decline has been underpinned by a problem of financing. What is needed is a method of raising all finance for locally provided services within the administrative area concerned. However, until this is discovered, Westminster and Whitehall will insist on having a say in the spending of the funds delivered from the Treasury to county and district level government. In the absence of a balance in funding arrangements, it is difficult to arrive at the correct balance between the influence of local and national interests.

Local government systems throughout Europe are differently financed from those in the UK, using a blend of local sales tax and local income tax. They also differ greatly in the mixture of devolution, deconcentration and decentralisation they possess. This in turn affects the politicisation or 'de-politicisation' of the police. In Germany, for example, the Police President is a party appointee. In the Netherlands procurators, police officers and burgomeisters are permitted to be party members and the distribution throughout the country of these officials reflects the vote gained by particular parties at particular times. The 'winner-take-all' system of the UK is now increasingly out of step with the system prevalent on the European continent which is based on proportional representation and the sharing out of the electoral spoils. This in turn has implications for the police. Under a proportional representation system the police service relates to all parties. The Police Commissioner/Chief of Police is thus aware of conflicting priorities and has the responsibility of aggregating the demands of different local interests into a coherent police policy. In the UK, a chief police officer can choose to ignore the demands of the party dominant at local level, because the officer's future depends on administering and implementing of the policies of the party dominant at national level. Either way, only one party has to be dealt with at a time. In the UK, a chief constable is increasingly an implementer of policy from above rather than an aggregator of policies from below.

Similar problems have been present in France. The Mitterrand socialist government introduced high degrees of decentralisation in an attempt to reduce the powers of the Préfet as the representative of national government, by increasing the power of the mayor and creating a municipal police with a positive relationship with the urban community. The relative power of national and local government over policing policy and strategy has been a constant source of political conflict in most European countries from 1800 onwards. The argument for localism and local accountability in policing is partly to do with a wish that the police enforce local rather than national priorities. While this may stem from a tradition of local policing preventing strangers becoming a burden on the local taxation system, it also reflects a wish by a community to have the police deal with crime against them rather than crimes committed by them.

Legitimacy, Discretion and the Uniform Police

Policing is not well served by standardised systems. Therefore legitimacy is not a uniform doctrine that is based on identical values in all parts of a country at any one time. Good policing consists of exercising discretion (Goldstein, 1960) and knowing which forms of behaviour are acceptable and unacceptable in specific areas. In Appeldoorn in the Netherlands, the Chief Constable told a visiting group that he would not tolerate coffee shops and that the local residents were very angry about them. However, in Amsterdam an off-duty police officer is quite likely to visit a coffee shop and enjoy its wares. Street parties and all-night parties may be tolerated in one area of the city and be extremely offensive in another. Displays of homosexual affection may be behaviour likely to cause a breach of the peace in some places and be perfectly normal behaviour in others. Increasingly it has become normal behaviour and should be tolerated as such, but the process through which the acceptability of homosexuality has been transformed has been difficult for the police, in terms of exercising their discretion. As the acceptability of other forms of behaviour changes in the future, whether they become more or less socially acceptable, they will equally become the focus of the exercise of police discretion.

The attitude of the police to warehouse parties and acid-house parties in the late 1980s was a bizarre abuse of police discretion and did not assist the relationship between the police and youth in the UK at that time. On the other hand, the police hid behind the then law and did not proceed against New Age Travellers trespassing on farmland, which did not help their relationship with landowners. Hunting, raves, festivals, road building and protest are all areas where the police have to use their discretion carefully and have to resist interference by national politicians pursuing votes from sections of the community.

All these issues are controversial in different ways in the countries of the EU, and to expect society to be uniform and to obey identical rules throughout Europe is to misunderstand the concept of the Europe of the regions. Harmonisation is thus a dangerous concept. Formal harmonisation in the area of discretion is particularly unlikely, although in any country a police officer observing two crimes being committed simultaneously by two different people has to choose which one to pursue. A police officer driving down the street will see a number of offences committed, and has to make exactly the same sort of choice. This involves the exercise of discretion. Yet although German police officers will exercise this form of discretion, the dominant German political culture lays stress on the notion of formal rules and such discretion is not officially sanctioned. However, this disparity between rulebook and practice underlines the importance of understanding that other cultures have different attitudes to policing.

Other police services in the past have laid stress on the mediation of disputes between citizens, rather than the declaration of fault and the prosecution of one or both parties. The public's expectation of how the police will behave in certain circumstances is in itself part of the system of informal rules. An outsider may find it very difficult to discover what these informal rule systems are, whether that outsider is an academic, a new police appointment or even judicial appointment to an area.

This in turn affects the response of the judicial authorities. Where the police do not have a dominant enforcement culture, the authorities treat seriously any case that is brought to court. Where the police have an excessive enforcement culture, the judicial authorities will treat offences brought to court lightly. Between these two extremes lies the police culture in which the police themselves can administer summary punishment, or at least have done so in the past, be it a beating, persecution by parking ticket, a system of cautioning, or a system of diversion from the judicial process. The police and the courts may compete for the power to administer diversion, but courts that are clogged by a heavy case load will benefit from the police ability to administer summary and trivial punishment. What is not known is the degree to which this is successful at deterrence and rehabilitation of offenders.

The police are thus part of the judicial system and there is a necessary relationship between that system and the police. Changing attitudes to the legitimacy of corporal punishment have reduced the options for the police and their ability to administer summary justice to a juvenile. Diversion from the criminal justice system to community service and re-education has replaced physical violence as a form of summary justice, but there must be a process by which diversion, as a form of justice, can be reviewed and legitimised by the community in which it is being administered. Judicial review, even by a system such as the Scottish Children's Panels, is preferable to decisions being taken by police officers without outside supervision.

Conclusion

Police exercise of discretion is crucial to both legitimacy and accountability. Research has shown it to be the most difficult aspect of police work for managers to supervise (Goldstein, 1963). All the elaborate frameworks of judicial and political accountability that characterise European police organisation can be rendered irrelevant if police officers refuse to enforce a particular law at street level. Equal Opportunities initiatives remain policies on paper if constables ignore them in practice. The Dutch attempt to make their police more representative of society by setting recruitment targets for women and ethnic groups is thus much more than an attempt to be politically correct. It is a recognition that police officers need to discard their white, racist, macho past by learning to work with women and ethnic minorities as equals.

6. Facilitating Cross-Border Co-operation

People wish to live in a Union in which their fundamental rights are fully respected. They wish to be able to live and to move freely within the Union, without fear of threats to their personal security. International crime transcends national borders within the Union. The Union must therefore be able to extend as necessary across those borders the protection of its citizens and the fight against international crime.

(Dublin II draft revision of Maastricht Treaty, December 1996)

Introduction

While previous chapters have raised factors militating against diversity, cross-border crime is the biggest single factor pushing police organisations in Europe towards uniformity.[1] Since the signing of the Single European Act in 1985, various arrangements have been introduced to cope with an anticipated growth in cross-border crime: a criminal may live in one country, commit a crime in a second and sell the goods stolen in a third, or groups of criminals in one country may set up links with groups in others to pursue various criminal enterprises.

The crime which most interests the Commission is fraud against the Community budget. To estimate the actual number of frauds, a minimum multiplier of three and a maximum of ten should be applied to the official figures of reported frauds (Tupman, 1994b). There may also be an accounting 'norm' for anticipated losses from fraudulent activity as a percentage of a large organisation's budget, against which the Commission's record could be measured. Similar calculations need to be carried out for the drugs trade, commodity smuggling, counterfeit products, antique theft, car theft and terrorism. These were the cross-border criminal activities that it was assumed would expand in the absence of regular border checks. Smuggling of people, commodities and counterfeit products are turning out to be more important in terms of value, while minor crimes are turning out to be more important in volume. Research into cross-border crime is necessary in order that the frameworks for cross-border police cooperation are appropriate and proportionate.

Both cross-border and supranational arrangements have been incorporated into European policing and this has been accompanied by a process of harmonisation of Justice and Home affairs procedures that has already been touched on in previous chapters. Although 'harmonisation' is primarily a German agenda, it is supported strongly by the Dutch, even though they are determined to maintain their own policy on drugs.

This chapter will review these cross-border and supranational arrangements, explaining where harmonisation has been a particular problem. Various cross-border policing initiatives have dominated the EU since the passing of the Single European Act. These are of three types: cross- and trans-national policing bodies, treaties and transnational policy-making bodies.

Steps are also being taken to facilitate cross-border investigation. To short-circuit legal problems of jurisdiction and procedure there has been a 'dash for telematics': an attempt to overcome politico-legal boundaries by exchanging information in 'cyberspace'. Apart from accountability, the central issue for cross-border investigation is that of turning information into intelligence and then into evidence. The legal problems of evidence admissibility raise five main issues:

- can police officers legally carry out surveillance in other countries, and if so, in which format should the evidence be submitted and what sort of supervision should there be of their activities?
- how can physical evidence from another country be obtained and analysed whilst preserving the chain of evidence?
- questions relating to the admissibility of evidence and requests for evidence from a computer screen;
- the problem of proving offence, intention to defraud and the existence of organisation, when the prime evidence is an Ana-Capa analysis of transactions between individuals and organisations;
- the problem of persuading witnesses to attend court in another country and, if they will not, of subjecting their evidence to cross-examination, where this is required.

Although the need to collect, analyse and share information lies behind the introduction of cross-national databases, their introduction has not settled these issues. Indeed in many ways it has highlighted them. The initiatives discussed below are but steps towards the formation of an environment for effective cross-national investigation and cannot be said actually to have achieved this. The proposals for a European *espace judiciaire* discussed in the next chapter may provide some solutions to the evidentiary problems outlined above.

Cooperation for what purpose?

The Single European Act forms the context within which cross-national policing is required; hence cooperation between police forces is driven by four main purposes:

- the investigation and successful prosecution of cross-border criminal enterprises;
- the safe handling of large movements of EU citizens across internal borders, such as football fans, tourists and demonstrations;
- uniform handling of entry to the EU of refugees, asylum-seekers, legal and illegal immigrants and 'undesirables', such as known international criminals;
- the handling of emergencies that require individual officers to cross borders, such as the hot pursuit of an individual caught in the act of committing an offence, or for a major disaster where numbers of officers are urgently needed for cordon duty, as auxiliary firefighters or in other roles.

Cooperation not only means the establishment of procedures but also implies the exchange of ideas and personnel for training courses and on-the-spot experience. Whilst ad hoc and individual arrangements between members of different police forces have always existed, these are not sufficient at an institutional level and cannot guarantee equality of treatment. Hence, there has been a search for an effective model for cross- and supra-national policing.

Competing Models of Cross-border Policing
Federal policing

A number of competing models are available for supranational arrangements. The Germans prefer an arrangement similar to that which was introduced in Germany by the Allies after 1945. In both Germany and the USA the system is facilitated by the separation of offences, one set of offences comprising a distinct criminal code for which the national force is responsible and other offences being the province of the local police. This is the central problem for the EU. To introduce a European Criminal Code implies a European legislature and European Courts. The UK has been the vanguard of resistance to this process, and, in fact, the criminal justice system of England and Wales is at odds with the basic principles of law held by the other systems, including that of Scotland. It is also suspected that, if the UK did not oppose the process so adamantly, France would have been equally opposed. The French accuse the Italians of having surrendered to the Dutch-German model in their recent reform, which removed judges/magistrati from their role in the investigative process and passed all power to the prosecutors.

The Germans, like the Americans, are accustomed to dealing with cross-border problems within their state boundaries. There is a set of legal and political arrangements for dealing with cooperation between Länder just as there are between the individual state and city police services in the USA. In both cases, as well as local units, there is a national organisation for criminal investigation: the FBI in the USA and the BKA in Germany. Just as the FBI became fascinated with the use of computer technology during the 1970s and 1980s (Poveda, 1990), so too did the Germans in their struggle with the Baader-Meinhof group and its terrorist off-shoots in the 1970s. The conclusion of this chapter will examine how far the EU has adopted computer technology to assist in criminal investigation.

Europol

The first attempt at establishing a transnational policing organisation to handle cross-border policing resulted in the setting-up of Europol. It is based on the Dutch CRI and Danish Central Intelligence Unit, which were also copied to some degree in the founding of their English equivalent, the National Crime Intelligence Service (NCIS). Here a group of officers gather and analyse information, but have no powers of arrest and have to rely on other branches of the domestic police to act operationally. Europol, prior to the Treaty of Amsterdam, was severely understaffed even for its residual data-gathering duties, and depended upon units based in each individual member state rather than the small group of officers resident in the Netherlands. It is easy to understand the Secretary-General of Interpol's bemusement as to why its tasks could not be performed by European bureaux within Interpol, if it were not intended to become operational. To understand the present status and future potential of Europol it is also necessary to examine the Treaties of Maastricht and Amsterdam. These, and their relevance to Europol, will be discussed later in the chapter.

Jealous protection of sovereignty seems the most likely explanation for the failure of Europol to follow the model of cooperation developed by Customs organisations. These have successfully set up joint operational teams with members drawn from each country involved in a case, on an ad hoc basis, but under protocols to the Treaty of Naples. The Europol Convention of 26 July 1995 created a body in danger of being characterised as a post-box plus computer. It does not have enough centrally-based staff to carry out analysis in the fashion of the Dutch CRI or the UK NCIS. Article 2 sets Europol the objectives of improving:

> the effectiveness and cooperation of the competent authorities in the Member States in preventing and combatting terrorism, unlawful drug trafficking and other serious forms of international crime where there are factual indications that an organised criminal structure is involved and two or more Member States are affected...in such a way as to require a common approach by the Member States owing to the scale, significance and consequences of the offences concerned. (OJEC 1995a:5)

Such a definition would seem to include fraud against the Community budget. There is potential here for conflict with the Unité pour Coordination de la Lutte Anti-Fraude (UCLAF), discussed below.

Initially, Europol was to concentrate on drugs, nuclear substances, trade in human beings and motor vehicle crime. Its next task was to deal with terrorism within two years. Article 2.3 gives Europol competence over money-laundering and related criminal offences, including offences 'committed in order to procure the means for perpetrating acts within the sphere of competence of Europol' and offences committed to ensure impunity of acts within Europol's competence. This must include fraud against the Community budget. Europol will act as an intelligence agency and will be database oriented.

To avoid some of the legal problems of evidence, jurisdiction and powers of arrest raised above, Europol is divided into national units and seconded liaison officers. Both are subject to the national law of the seconding member state. Certain exceptions in the case of the liaison officer are specified by the Convention, largely having to do with data protection, although a further protocol with regard to Europol's privileges and immunities is awaited. This, prior to the Treaty of Amsterdam, was a long way from a European FBI and weaker than the UCLAF model.

UCLAF

The closest approach to embodying a European FBI has been made by the Unité pour Coordination de la Lutte Anti-Fraude, the organisation within the European Commission concerned with preventing fraud against the European budget. UCLAF has the advantage of serving one master, unlike Schengen's 13 (plus two non-EU 'observers', Iceland and Norway) or Europol's 15. It also has the advantage of dealing with a single crime and has a determination to establish links with a single partner organisation in each Member State.

UCLAF represents a more radical approach to investigative cooperation. The Commission reorganised its own anti-fraud units by its communiqué of 4 November, 1992 (Tupman, 1994b). A further reform took place in 1995, virtually unifying the staffs (SEC, 1995). A total of 138 staff work in the main units and the European Parliament has passed an amendment to provide 50 further staff.

UCLAF does not have the power to arrest and question suspects, to search premises and seize documents, or to compel potential witnesses to attend and answer questions or supply documents. It does have the power to request that investigations be carried out by the competent services of the Member States involved. It may also take the lead when effective investigation of a case demands coordination between Member States (UCLAF, 1996).

Models of the type of Member State unit with which UCLAF finds it efficient to work are Belgium's OCDEFO (Central Office for the Prevention of Organised Economic and Financial Crime) and Italy's Guardia di Finanza. The former is a good example of inter-agency work, consisting of customs and taxation investigators working with prosecutors and police officers. The latter now has a unit attached to the Prime Minister's department for the coordination of Community policies which is presumably satisfactory as long as the Prime Minister is not corrupt. What is required appears to be a single body through which the work of other in-country bodies can be coordinated, so that UCLAF only has to deal with one body in each member state. This body must itself be administratively prestigious with connections with authorities sufficiently elevated to ensure that investigations are given priority on a basis other than that normally followed domestically.

Politicians from those Member States that resist strengthening supranational investigative structures maintain that the Commission is exploiting the issue of fraud against the Communities' financial interest; using it as the thin end of the wedge of a policy to set up its own police and further erode national sovereignty. The 'cui bono' test, however, applies to both sides. If organised crime is involved to the extent suggested by UCLAF's intelligence analysis, then corruption must also be a serious possibility. The allegations against senior Italian politicians and the recent case against an equally senior Belgian politician must raise the possibility that corruption is a factor in the reluctance of some institutions at Member State level to pursue fraud against the Community budget. A Protocol on Corruption was in preparation in December 1995 and was expected to be adopted after consultation with the European Parliament during 1996, but this was one of many pieces of legislation to fall foul of the then UK Conservative Government's 'mad cow' boycott (FAF, 1995:18).

The Impact Of Treaties
The Treaty of Maastricht
It was considered that cross-border crime was already spreading in advance of any change in border-controls and that different approaches were necessary. The declaration on Police cooperation from the Treaty stated that the Member States, '...are

willing to envisage the adoption of practical measures ... relating to the following functions'. Those relevant to this chapter are 'Creation of Databases' and 'Central analysis and assessment of information in order to take stock of the situation and identify investigative approaches'.

Elsewhere in the Treaty, Article K, the surprise article in the Treaty of Maastricht, covered cooperation in the fields of justice and home affairs. K1 sets out nine areas of common interest :

- asylum policy;
- crossing external borders and controls thereon;
- immigration policy and policy regarding third country nationals;
- combating drug addiction;
- combating fraud;
- judicial cooperation in civil matters;
- judicial cooperation in criminal matters;
- customs cooperation;
- police co-operation on terrorism, drug trafficking and other serious forms of international crime including if necessary customs co-operation, 'In connection with the organisation of a union wide system for exchanging information within a European Police Office (Euro Pol)'.

K2 brings in the principles laid down by the European Convention for the Protection of Human Rights and Fundamentals of 4 November 1950 and the Convention relating to the Status of Refugees of 28 July 1951, as laying down basic principles for dealing with the matters referred to above.

K3 provides for the initiative of any member of the state or of the Commission in the areas referred to in article K1(1.2.6), as well as providing for article K1(7.2.9) as being only on the initiative of any member state.

In addition, a new article 3 raises a whole series of areas that will affect police work and law enforcement generally. 3F, for example, provides for a common policy in the sphere of transport. A close examination of the terms of DRIVE 2000, Directorate General XIII's plan for the application of information technology to transport policy, demonstrated that law enforcement is part of the package. The logic of its argument was that accidents and breakdowns slow the free movement of goods and people; therefore, cars and lorries must be properly maintained and this must be enforced.

3H refers to 'the approximation of the laws of Member States to the extent required of the functioning of the common market'.

3K provides for a policy in the sphere of the environment and 3S provides for a contribution to the strengthening of consumer protection.

K4 creates a commission of senior civil servants of Member States to produce practical policies for all these areas. This will prepare the Council's discussions in the areas referred to in K1 and decision-making shall be 'unanimous except in matters of procedure and in cases where article K3 expressly provides for other voting rules'.

All these articles delineated, in effect, areas for the creation of databases and software to produce pattern analysis and offender profiling. This was seen as the central policy response to the new situation, involving the absence of borders, since resource shortages and the sheer number of people and goods crossing borders made it no longer possible to stop and check everybody. Efficient use of resources thus demands that only the occasional random spot check takes place. Therefore a system has to be developed for maximising the effectiveness of the spot check and minimising the amount of inconvenience to people not being checked. Exchange of information between Member States, direct police co-operation at the sharp end, as opposed to the policy end, and applications of USA-style crime offender profiling, are seen as the only likely ways of increasing the efficiency of those checks that are allowed. There is also a need to create a European Crime Intelligence System that will permit police officers to carry out cross-border surveillance and transfer the surveillance of potential offenders from one force to another.

The Treaty of Amsterdam

As Member States made their submissions to the 1996 Intergovernmental Conference (IGC) preparing what became the Treaty of Amsterdam, they reviewed several possible models of supranational policy-making in the justice and home affairs arena, not all of which may be compatible with effective cross-border investigative cooperation.[2] Many are represented among the existing patchwork of European institutions. The simplest, a Directorate for Justice and Home Affairs within the Commission, presented many Member States with serious problems. Without a Directorate, a European Criminal Code and a European FBI appeared a distant prospect.

Existing policy-making structures are competitive and contradictory. This has its roots to some degree in the post-war continental European resistance to centralisation in the field of policing policy, arising out of the totalitarian experience of the Second World War. Nevertheless, the involvement of the Ministries of Justice, the Interior, Defence, and in the case of fraud and customs duties, Finance, for each of the 15 Member States, makes for a long, drawn-out policy-making process, involving some 60 different units which must achieve unanimity. Indeed it is surprising that any progress has been made at all.

The reforms made by the Treaty of Amsterdam in the Third Pillar area, which deals with Justice and Home affairs decided on an intergovernmental basis, were unanticipated. An examination of the European Parliament's briefings on the lead-up to the IGC, which covered all the Member States' political positions, shows no majority, let alone a consensus for the reforms that eventually emerged (EUROPARL).

The Treaty fundamentally revised Title VI, which essentially governed Third Pillar matters. Articles K 1 - 14 of the Treaty of Maastricht have become articles 29 - 42 of the Treaty of Amsterdam, under Title VI, which is now titled *Provisions on Police and Judicial Cooperation in Criminal Matters*. Articles K15 - 17 of the Treaty of Maastricht are now articles 43 - 45 in the Treaty of Amsterdam, under Title VII, *Provisions on Closer Cooperation*.

Amsterdam shifted some of the work designated Third Pillar, into the First Pillar, the Community sphere. Everything to do with the crossing of external borders, immigration and judicial cooperation on civil matters will have been incorporated into the Community sphere by 2001 and subject to qualified majority voting, leading to 'more and quicker decisions' (Amsterdam, Q22). Criminal matters have been left to the cooperation of the police, governments and civil services within a more legally binding and effective system. Fraud and customs cooperation will also come under qualified majority voting. Thus, of the nine areas of common interest set out in article K1 of the Treaty of Maastricht, only three, K.1.4 (combating drug addiction), K.1.7 (judicial cooperation in criminal matters) and K.1.9 (police cooperation on terrorism, drug trafficking and other serious forms of international crime), remain Third Pillar matters. Research and technological development go to the First Pillar, too, which means that Information Technology policy will be a matter of First Pillar decision-making procedures.

The K4 Commission, established by the Treaty of Maastricht and including the UK and Ireland, was originally seen as shadowy and potentially hugely powerful, because of its right to make proposals directly to Council. It included the 15 Member States, plus Malta and Cyprus as observers. Several submissions to the 1996 IGC surprisingly depicted K4 as a huge disappointment (EUROPA, 1995a). The Reflection Group proposed a proper Work Programme for K4 as an essential next step.

The K4 Commission nearly became the K8 Commission under the new Treaty. It will now need further renaming. Article K8 is now Article 36 in the consolidated version of the Treaty.

K4 superceded TREVI (a group named after the famous fountain, which could be seen from the conference room in which it first met), a body at which senior European police officers were allowed by their political and administrative masters to meet, discuss matters of common concern and even suggest ways of harmonising policy. After years of being little more than a dining club (Interviews, 1991), TREVI began to propose detailed policies, first on terrorism, then on training and other matters relating to the anticipated consequences of the abolition of internal borders on 1 January 1993. It also facilitated networking amongst senior police officers. The TREVI organisers made the serious political mistake of restricting the Commission's representation. K4 puts power firmly back in the hands of civil servants, but the criticisms voiced suggest that this may have prevented necessary progress. K4 was intended to be a body tasked with proposing initiatives to coordinate national policies, investigative units and legal systems, with special regard to the areas outlined by article K1. Civil servants are good at administering policy made by others, but are not empowered to take initiatives. A successful policy-making body either needs to be composed of politicians or sharp-end practitioners.

Article 30 (new K2) states:

> Common action in the field of police cooperation shall include:...the collection, storage, processing, analysis and exchange of relevant information, including information held by law enforcement services on reports on suspicious financial transactions, in particular through Europol, subject to appropriate provisions on the protection of personal data.

Schengen Agreement

Schengen is not a Treaty, but an Agreement (1985), followed by a Convention (1990) and developed into a series of working practices, all of which together comprise the

Schengen Acquis. It began as an attempt to overcome perceived problems that would arise from 1 January 1993 as a consequence of the Single European Act. Most Member States anticipated that the 'four fundamental freedoms'; the free movement of goods, capital, services and persons (EUROPARL 27), implied the removal of border controls by all Member States. As a result, something was needed to ensure that the borders became open for police services but not for criminals. Until it was incorporated into the Treaties of European Union under the Treaty of Amsterdam, Schengen was driven by the five original signatories, Germany, Benelux and France, which allowed it to maintain a surprising level of momentum. Spain and Portugal had achieved decision-maker status prior to incorporation, but Italy and Greece had some way to go in catching up the core group. On 16 June 1995, the Nordic Union states reached agreement with Schengen. Denmark, Finland and Sweden became full members and Norway and Iceland as non-EU members became associate members (Statewatch, 1995). On incorporation, the UK and Ireland were given an opt-out arrangement. Denmark was also given recognition of its special position. For reasons that will become clear later, the Commission also has to negotiate a Treaty with Iceland and Norway, non-members of the EU, but parties to Schengen.

Even in those countries that are party to Schengen, bilateral arrangements predominate over all-Schengen arrangements. The Länder system meant that the Germans found it relatively easy to set up bilateral arrangements for cross-border cooperation under the Schengen agreement. Schleswig-Holstein Land dealt directly with Denmark; the Netherlands borders two Länder only - Nordrein-Westphalia and Niedersachsen; Belgium, one - Nordrein-Westphalia again; Luxemburg, one - Rheinland Pfalz; and France, three - Baden-Würtemburg and Rheinland Pfalz as well as the smaller Land of Saarland. The other Schengen partners had to establish a counterpart for the purpose of negotiating what were at first ad hoc arrangements, but slowly developed into frameworks within which bilateral cross-border cooperation now takes place. The Dutch reform to county-style forces greatly reduced the number of units with a border with another country and the Belgian partial reform at least made the Gendarmerie responsible for all cross-border matters, although the Police Municipale individually make informal contacts with their neighbours. Similarly, before reunification, Bavaria could deal with Austria. Even after reunification, only Poland had the difficulty of bordering several Länder.

France, with its centralised approach, posed the only problem, but had no difficulty setting up appropriate multi-agency committees of police, gendarmes, judges and prefects. All other relationships were state-to-state. Spain only had France to deal with; Portugal, only Spain; Italy, France on one frontier and Austria on the other. The Scandinavians, like Benelux, had already set up free travel areas, as of course had the UK and Ireland. The Scandinavian problem was solved by bringing Norway and Iceland into the Schengen agreement, leaving only Greenland as an anomaly. The UK/Ireland free travel area means that Ireland cannot join Schengen nor declare open borders with the rest of the EU as long as the UK refuses to do so.

The Commission, which is represented at Schengen decision-making meetings, might explore the possibility of extending the Schengen goals to include compatibility of approach to fraud against the Community Budget. In particular, the concept of representing all relevant internal bodies with an investigative role could be transferred to create supranational panels of judges/procurators from relevant jurisdictions to play an ad hoc role in individual investigations and ultimately, in the absence of a European Criminal Court, to try particular cross-border cases on an individual basis.

The Schengen agreements only cover procedures to be adopted to replace checks on individuals after opening borders. Checks on luggage and goods were left to the European Community as a whole to decide. The Convention thus covers:

- surveillance of external frontiers;
- harmonisation of visa policies;
- freedom of movement of aliens;
- criteria for designating the country responsible for processing an application for asylum;
- cooperation between police forces;
- cooperation between the legal authorities in matters covered by criminal law;
- extradition;
- delegation of responsibility for enforcing criminal judgements;
- narcotics;
- firearms and ammunition.

Schengen and Amsterdam

Protocol 1 of the Treaty of Amsterdam incorporates the *Schengen Acquis*. The new applicants will not be able to opt out but have to satisfy its requirements in full as a precondition of entry.

Title VII of the Treaty of Amsterdam permits in effect the creation of a new super Schengenland, if a majority of Member States become disillusioned with the progress of cooperation. It would be possible, under its provisions, to set up networked criminal databases, interrogatable from any participant country, if a small number of states found such a step legally or politically unacceptable.

The creation of the SIRENE bureaux (Supplement d'Information Requis à l'Entree Nationale), as a compromise between information technology and judicial supervision to expedite the old commission rogatoire system, needs evaluation to see if there are principles that can be applied elsewhere, especially as SIRENE Phase 2 has begun (Tupman, 1995a). Cross-border surveillance operations and extraterritorial police operations in general, under appropriate judicial supervision, have been legitimised. The principles involved could presumably be extended to UCLAF operatives. The Commission, historically represented at Schengen decision-making meetings, might explore the possibility of extending the Schengen goals to include compatibility of approach to fraud against the Community Budget.

The Schengen Information System appears to be up and fully running. It has absorbed the projected European Information System (Statewatch), now that the Acquis is incorporated and that the UK and Ireland can choose to cooperate with some aspects of the Acquis but not all.

Amsterdam and Europol

As stated above, prior to Amsterdam, not only was there potential for conflict between UCLAF and Europol in the area of fraud, but the latter was also significantly weaker than UCLAF and had no prospect of acting as a European FBI. The Commission ordered the two to work together in the 1997 UCLAF work plan. More general problems were at least partially addressed by the Treaty of Amsterdam. Article K.2.2 obliges the Council to *promote cooperation through Europol* [authors' italics] and, within five years after Amsterdam enters into force, the Council must:

> enable Europol to facilitate and support the preparation, and to encourage the coordination and carrying out, of specific investigative actions by the competent authorities of the Member States, including operational actions of joint teams comprising representatives of Europol in a support capacity;

> adopt measure allowing Europol to ask the competent authorities of the Member States to conduct and coordinate their investigations in specific cases and to develop specific expertise which may be put at the disposal of Member States to assist them in investigating cases of organised crime;

> promote liaison arrangements between prosecuting/investigating officials specialising in the fight against organised crime in cooperation with Europol;

> establish a research, documentation and statistical network on cross-border crime.

Although the present authors remain suspicious of the likelihood of manpower resources being delivered to Europol, the organisation finally seems to be following UCLAF's more radical approach to investigative cooperation. K 13.3 lays down financial procedures - administrative expenditure shall be charged to the Community budget, as shall operational expenditure, except where the Council decides otherwise, in which case it shall be charged to the Member States in accordance with the GNP scale, unless Council unanimously decides otherwise.

The Database Strategy

In default of a European FBI, all attempts at cross-border police organisation since 1985 have centred on the creation of a networked computer database. A number of such cross-border databases and database-related communication systems have now been established as necessary prerequisites for risk-assessment together with offender and offence profiling. Their advantages are:

- offender profiling is vital for identifying individuals and organisations who commit relevant types of offence - fraud, smuggling, trade in people;
- offence profiling ensures that investigators are up-to-date with the modus operandi of the various offences being committed and with the organisational structures required to commit them;
- risk-assessment enables proper targetting of scarce resources, both for prevention and successful investigation;

- information technology enables rapid exchange of relevant intelligence between investigative organisations across frontiers and removes bureaucratic obstacles with regard to provision of evidence. At the same time officers remain accountable to existing command structures.

All cross-national database schemes have had problems achieving their original goals. The major problems have been:
- compatibility between EU Member States' software and hardware;
- judicial acceptability of on-screen communication in place of paper;
- data-protection and privacy;
- analytical software for profiling;
- consistency of reporting of offences by individual countries and organisations.

The Schengen Information System (SIS) has been transformed into a man-machine interface by the SIRENE bureaux. The former's original anti-immigration aspect has recently been transferred to the proposed database Eurodac.

The European Commission's own investigative organisation, UCLAF, assists Member States to focus on high risk areas by providing information resulting from an analysis of information on its databases: - pre-IRENE (IRégularities, ENquêtes et Exploitation), for cases of fraud under investigation and IRENE, for cases successfully investigated. These were combined to create IRENE 95, another step towards upgrading the system from an electronic filing cabinet to a full-scale independent knowledge-based system that can identify and analyse risk factors. IRENE has had many problems in gestation, but now includes over 20,000 cases.

The other major relevant databases are DAF (Database Anti-Fraud), SCENT (System Customs ENforcement Network), and CIS (Customs Information System). There are now 323 SCENT/CIS terminals installed at airports and administrative headquarters. They may be used to record and to access data on both Community and non-Community matters. With regard to CIS, European Union Member States have adopted a convention on the use of information systems in the customs field. Agreement has also been reached on the provisional application of this convention between some of the Member States. The convention itself has not yet been ratified, so the central database cannot yet be created. Without further research, it is impossible to say whether there is deliberate obstruction on the part of some Member States, or if some have a technology problem.

On 26 July 1995, under article K3 of the Treaty of Maastricht, a Convention was signed on the use of information technology for customs purposes. It provides a legal basis for including in a database information to combat drug-trafficking. This database is being set up. In addition, the system for registration of goods in transit across the EU is being computerised, in cooperation with EFTA: 'Although it is obvious that computerisation will not totally wipe out fraud, it is safe to assume that the cost of this project will soon be recouped'.

This view is belied by the development of every computer system. It is not safe to assume costs will be recouped. It is safer to assume that the system will not do what the client originally thought it would. What it does may be useful but will not be as per specification. The databases so far established in the European Union have been good at recording data, but poor at analysis, and have run into data-protection and judicial supervision problems that have reduced them to electronic filing-systems of limited utility as investigative tools. Nevertheless they continue to proliferate. The Europol Convention is 75 per cent concerned with database matters. It is time for serious analysis of investigator use of databases in order to establish how successful they have been in achieving their original goals, to identify good practice and to establish real costs. Above all, a project needs to be established to examine and overcome the legal and technological problems of moving from a primitive man-machine interface to intelligent, analysis-capable software.

An intelligence- and database-oriented approach is unlikely to be successful if information is slow to reach database managers because of bureaucratic delay and complexity. To by-pass obstacles, UCLAF proposed the installation of 'an experimental freephone service to allow European citizens to provide information on fraud in confidence directly to the Commission'. The freephone number received over 4,000 calls in the first 12 months of its operation from November 1995. Around 200 of these led to further investigations and subsequent formal enquiries involved amounts of over 30 million ECUs .

Equally important, if databases are to provide a true picture, is the issue of notification. A targeted strategy demands reliable, up-to-date information. A Commission proposal to improve both the level of detail and frequency of submission of Member States' reports of fraud and irregularities was due to be adopted during 1996. The intriguing question is how long it can be before banks and financial institutions are also placed under legal obligation to report fraud to a central database. The impact of a database-led strategy will be affected by the priorities of individual countries. Investigative priority will be determined by the perceived scale of the problem and this is normally measured on a purely financial basis. Article 209a of the Treaty of Maastricht establishes 'the assimilation principle', whereby Member States shall take the same measures to counter fraud affecting the Community as they take to counter fraud affecting themselves. In the UK this may be counter-productive - officers from the Serious Fraud Office have told the authors privately that they do not investigate frauds below £5million. This is because of the immense costs of prosecution. Presumably, local fraud squads, Ministry of Agriculture, Food and Fisheries inspectors and Inland Revenue officials operate to different guidelines. Recognising this problem, the Convention on the Protection of the European Communities Financial Interests of 26 July 1995 instructs Member States to define serious fraud as involving a minimum amount that cannot be set at less than 50,000 ECUs. Legislators may define an offence as serious by using financial criteria, but investigative priority cannot be guaranteed where there is already a heavy domestic case-load that is being prioritised on the basis of higher monetary value.

As long as the policing of cross-border crime is hamstrung by governments' reluctance to set up a permanent cross-border police organisation, idiotically complex sets of regulations will continue to be passed. The new draft Treaty, if passed, will take a further step away from the present impasse by empowering Europol to set up joint investigative teams for individual operations. Customs organisations can already do this, so there is a precedent and this may produce a more effective halfway house.

The new draft Treaty and Conventions already in place confront most of these issues at a high policy level. The Customs network, finance ministry-driven and concentrating on drug smuggling and revenue evasion, is the most successful integrator of information technology and joint investigation teams. Europol has too many potential responsibilities and suffers from in-fighting between the Ministries of the Interior and Justice, which has prevented the K4 Commission from developing into a successful driver of policy. The Schengen system has made progress but moved away from its original, information technology-driven, vision.

As argued earlier, UCLAF, responsible directly to the Commission, free of the multi-national decision-making process and single-crime oriented, is the only supranational body capable of driving cross-border investigative policy and practice forward. The organised crime groups it investigates are involved in many other types of crime outside its competence. It will of necessity exceed any brief it is given. While this should be welcomed if it increases the effectiveness of the battle against organised crime, it will inevitably be portrayed as part of the battle for sovereignty between the Commission and certain Member States.

Conclusion

The simplest way forward for policy making would be a Directorate for Justice and Home Affairs within the Commission. The varying lack of priority given by Member States will affect the success or failure of cross-border cooperation and is a fundamental obstacle to obtaining compatibility of approach by the Member States. The perceived scale of the problem will determine investigative priority and this is normally measured on a purely financial basis. Cross-border crime is primarily not a problem of economics, but of political confidence. The supporters of the European Union and the Single Market cannot afford a situation to arise where the abolition of borders is perceived as a cause of an increase in crime, especially crime committed by foreigners.

If, for example, the Serious Fraud Office (SFO) in the UK do not investigate frauds below £5million and UCLAF is trying to operate through the SFO/Department of Trade and Industry interface, it may not be dealing with sums large enough to engage their interest, and they will be able to demonstrate that this is perfectly compatible with the assimilation principle established in article 209a of the Treaty of Maastricht.

Principles established by the Commission in one area have a habit of being applied elsewhere, so the assimilation principle may well become applicable in other areas of cross-border crime and raise similar problems. Similarly the example of UCLAF, as a model for cross-border investigation, may be taken up as a model in other areas of police activity. Internal bodies with an investigative role could be transferred to create supranational panels of judges/procurators from relevant jurisdictions.

While the paper whirls at intergovernmental level, the real drivers of policy, the criminals and the police, are working away. It is easy to forget that protocols on police procedure only represent an armistice, never a final settlement. Criminals change their modus operandi to circumvent the lawyers' beautifully crafted phrases and the police do likewise to bring them to justice. Whatever governments pronounce on the subject of sovereignty, police investigators create their own cross-border networks and find ways to assist each other. Some aspects of Schengen would have been required even without the Single European Act, because police surveillance units were already operating extraterritorially. Ministries of Justice end up legitimating effective police practice, rarely, if ever, determining it.

The demands for police cooperation produced by the growth in cross-border crime open an argument about what should remain of the diversity that has hitherto characterised European policing. There are strong arguments that criminals can use this diversity to avoid prosecution. It is therefore the structures discussed in Chapter 2 that are most under threat and that will be pushed towards uniformity. The Corpus juris proposals already incorporate an idea as to how the relationship between prosecutor, judge and police investigator should develop. However, the problem remains - should the laws being enforced now become the same throughout Europe and should they be enforced everywhere in the same way? The arguments about discretion, reviewed in the final sections of Chapters 3 and 4, are relevant here. Different communities wish to stay different. Society is becoming multicultural. A uniform police response, structured by a single Weberian hierarchy, is likely to create more conflict and more disorder than it can cope with. These arguments will be further developed in the final chapter.

1   This chapter rests heavily on work already published in the Hume Policy Papers (Tupman 1996), *The Journal of Financial Crime* (Tupman 1997b) and the *Journal of Information and Communications Technology Law* (Tupman 1998). The authors acknowledge the permission of Carfax Publishers to use it here.
2   A collection of these documents is available on the Internet together with the consolidated Treaty.

7. Harmonisation, Diversity and Processes of Reform

Introduction

The theme of this book has been that there is considerably more uniformity in policing processes and structures in Europe than might be appreciated by the English reader. The drive for effective cross-national policing, outlined in the previous chapter, has also highlighted the need for harmonisation of policing procedures. Equally, for investigation and prosecution to be effective, legal procedures must be drawn into that process of harmonisation. At the same time, individual countries wish to keep their own internal policies towards various crimes. There are therefore not only pressures for uniformity but also for diversity. In the light of the harmonisation project, the questions that must be confronted are, how strong are the pressures for uniformity? How much diversity is likely to remain at the end of the process? These questions are addressed in this chapter, which begins with a review of the various systems of classification offered by previous chapters. There follows a discussion of the different levels of policing that are emerging, which presents a final framework for analysing future developments and understanding the interplay of uniformity and diversity. There is then a discussion of how the argument for a European FBI may be illusory and an outline of the corpus juris proposals for a European *espace judiciaire,* which is potentially the most exciting development for European Policing in the near future.

This book began by suggesting that European policing systems can be divided into three types - Napoleonic, national and decentralised. In the second chapter, nine traditions of policing were distinguished. In the third, three models of criminal investigation were laid out. In the fourth, five systems of crowd management were presented. In the fifth, a multiplicity of mechanisms for legitimacy and accountability were discussed. The sixth suggested that, even at the supranational level, there are competing candidates for future cross-border cooperation.

Given this, can the proposition be sustained that there is more uniformity than diversity in European policing? Certainly, in terms of day-to-day police work, it can. The tyranny of the control room and the patrol car are the reality of the police constable at work. Detectives search for evidence in the same way; interviewing witnesses, waiting for the forensic scientist to offer analysis that may or may not be evidence and increasingly making entries on databases, or asking those databases for information. Rank structures are changing under pressure from management doctrine. 'Flattening the hierarchy' is the dominant slogan, reducing the numbers of ranks to three major roles: constable, supervisor and policy-maker.

Reviewing the three categories from the model from Chapter 1, the Napoleonic model is redundant. Unless widespread social dislocation is coming, with rising unemployment, strikes and confrontations, a paramilitary force is no longer required in the aftermath of the Cold War. The cities require the resources, and flexible deployment is the watchword of the day. Competition for the future is between the national model, the German decentralised model and the county model. Movement is taking place from the county to the national model (Sweden, Finland, and perhaps Scotland); from the Napoleonic to the national (Greece), and from the Napoleonic to the county (Netherlands and perhaps Belgium). Given the size of some German Länder, e.g. Nordrhein-Westphalia with a population of 30 million, a compromise is possible, whereby smaller countries adopt a national model, thereby becoming equivalent to German Länder. But the pressure for the future is towards a Basic Command Unit, with a policy-making budget-holder in charge of deployments. The structures above that level will remain diverse, but the reality will be a functionally-determined uniformity.

Into the model from Chapter 2 was built the idea that most sources of difference between the frameworks in which policing is carried out are historical and redundant. Crime and social disorder increasingly follow similar patterns across Europe. Homogenisation is as much the name of the game as harmonisation. Those differences that remain are largely sources of unecessary expense, and in a period when public expenditure is increasingly under pressure, will be increasingly difficult to defend.

Chapter 3 suggested that the English system of court procedure was becoming universal for serious crime, while the French and German systems are battling for supremacy at the lower courts. A possible further compromise is likely to be the introduction of a role for examining magistrates to oversee the rights of the accused in the judicial process, on the lines of the corpus juris proposals. This would leave the prosecutor to supervise investigation. It may be utopian to imagine that a system combining the best features of all models is emerging, but any compromise has to provide a role for advocates, prosecutors and magistrates. This really has little to do with day-to-day policing, even for the detective, so again apparent diversity has little actual impact on the uniformity of police practices.

Chapter 4 suggested that the uniform police really were uniform in terms of their day-to-day activity; differences came in the demands of crowd management. Even here, the reality increasingly is flame-proof clothing, helmets with visors, shields and batons. The demand that police officers be capable both of paramilitarism and of providing a friendly service to the community is inherently schizophrenic. Yet that was built into Rowan and Mayne's New Police from their inception. It is merely that the technology of non-lethality is a little more complex today. The future will be detemined by the realities of social conflict and the ability of police officers to buy time for politicians to take appropriate decisions. This will all depend on the success or failure of the grand European project and the problems that will be imported by the Agenda 2000 programme.

Chapter 5 examined the interplay between legitimacy, accountability and police discretion. Ultimately, the Dutch solution is likely to prevail. The police must be a microcosm of society, in order to exercise discretion in a legitimate way. As the pattern of crime and conflict homogenises across Europe, with environmental, gender and multicultural issues coming to the fore, police forces will have to become less white, male and macho. Mechanisms of political and judicial accountability will have to become more transparent, and the separation of police officers from political activity will become more and more difficult to justify.

Chapter 6 suggested further pressures towards uniformity. If criminals can ignore boundaries and transform themselves into networks, albeit of illegal European businessmen, some police officers at least are pushed down the same road, operating in many cities in different countries, in a variety of languages. Problems of evidence admissibility are an enormous factor pushing towards harmonisation of criminal justice systems. The same processes as those discussed in Chapter 3 are at work, creating pressures for compromise between German and French models of judicial process.

Balancing Uniformity and Diversity — a Framework for Understanding Future Development

This review puts the functional case for uniformity. In a Europe characterised by freedom of movement for people, goods and capital, there will be pressure for identical treatment of identical behaviour. If locals and visitors are treated differently, then this is akin to market-rigging in favour of locals. Against this, in a multicultural Europe, it will be argued strongly that cultural and religious diversity must be encouraged and that police officers will have to deal sensitively with behaviour that might constitute a breach of public order if carried out in one community, but be merely seen as a good party in another. There is still room for structural diversity.

In the Scarman Report, there was argument over whether it is possible or fair to police different communities differently. In fact, as already discussed in Chapter 5, most police forces give their officers some form of discretion and thus in practice policing is carried out differently at different times and in different circumstances. Given the existence of discretion, the nature of the officer exercising it becomes important. A female officer, for example may differ sharply from a male officer in her attitude to violence in the family. Equally, officers of West Indian or Asian origin will see matters differently from their ethnically English counterparts. The Dutch and Americans argue that the only way to even out the exercise of discretion is for the personnel of the police to reflect the composition of society.

As well as acknowledging the diversity of police officers, the recognition that there are different types of community to be policed, and different communities of interest to be served, leads to the conclusion that policing itself may need to be reorganised. It may well be that Europe is moving towards a hierarchy of police forces. Firstly, there is strong citizen demand throughout Europe for a foot patrol service with a responsibility for crime prevention and dealing with petty crime. This service needs to be accountable directly to the local community. It could be supplied by a private company, by the community itself, or by a local police service. The community here, however, needs to be at a level lower than a municipality, and any geographic community so defined will necessarily contain many others, whether these be communities of age, sexual preference, or ethnicity. Defining the sorts of community that would be served by a foot patrol service within a city will be a difficult process, but one that needs to be confronted before the 21st century gets too far underway. In commercial centres such an organisation is being created by default, and is supplied from the private sector. Some residential estates have also funded their own patrol. Hospital Trusts in the UK have provided funding to the local police service for a constable to patrol the public areas.

The second level required is for a police force that can provide both an emergency response and a public order capacity. This has to be funded by and accountable to a municipality or a provincial authority, depending on local government structure. Such a service will wear uniform and react to telephone calls and control room instructions. The problem would lie in the interface with the community-owned foot patrol service, which will end up dealing with the following-up of less serious calls. The introduction of personal radios and motorised patrol has already effectively converted many European police services into such organisations, responsible to the state rather than the community. This has created a legitimacy gap, in that the investigation of petty crime and crime prevention patrol have effectively been abandoned. Ordinary citizens

Type of policing	Aim	Accountability	Supply
Foot patrol	Crime prevention and investigation of petty crime	Local community	Private companies or local police or vigilantes
Rapid response	Emergencies and public order	Municipal or Provincial authority	uniform police could be gendarmerie
Criminal investigatiom	Serious crime: rape murder fraud	Ministry of Justice and Procuracy	Plain clothes detectives and interagency groups
Supranational	Cross-border crime; drug trafficking, terrorism. Money laundering, duty evasion	European Court of Justice, European Ministere Public. Committee of European Parliament	Customs, UCLAF, Europol
Multi-national	International Assistance	United Nations	Secondment from all sectors and contract basis from private sector

Table XVIII. Who will police what in the New Europe?

have been left without the service they require to deal with their immediate sources of insecurity.

Thirdly, there is a demand for a criminal investigation force to deal with serious crime. This involves crimes that carry lengthy sentences because they are viewed by society as particularly serious, such as rape and murder. However, as discussed in Chapter 2, it also involves crimes that are particularly complex to investigate or require special equipment or expertise, such as fraud. Such a force will be funded at national level and be responsible through appropriate judicial authorities to the Ministry of Justice.

Fourthly, as discussed in Chapter 4, the existence of cross-border crime has led to demand for either a national (where the country is big enough), or a super-national force (where a number of countries exist in close geographical proximity), to deal with problems related to drug trafficking, terrorism and organised crime, especially where this involves large-scale fraud and money laundering.

Fifthly, there is increasing demand for trained units to be available to assist the less developed countries in special circumstances such as major emergencies, disasters and inter-communal strife. Agenda 2000 and the admission of the first wave of former Communist countries has led to a particular demand for personnel to provide assistance in bringing the police services of these countries up to Schengen standard, as well as to a standard where they are enforcing the rule of law in a manner consistent with a democratic system. Table XVIII summarises these points.

If the processes at work in Europe have been correctly identified, then it should be possible to balance diversity at the lowest level of policing with uniformity of technology and standards of investigation at higher levels. Problems will arise, because of the changing nature of the demography of the European Union. An ageing population will continue to require immigration, to supply the workforce to provide the tax base that will support it at the standard to which it has become accustomed, and Eastern European communities will join the immigrants of the 1950s and 1960s. The expectations of the elderly, native population with a high fear of crime will have to be balanced against totally different expectations of police behaviour on the part of the new communities. This will create problems for systems of accountability and ethical conflicts for police officers.

The illusion of demands for an FBI

As discussed in the previous chapter, a whole series of arrangements have now been created that aspire to identify, investigate and facilitate prosecution of cross-border criminal activity - Schengen, UCLAF, Europol, Interpol's European Bureau, Customs arrangements under MAG 92, the K4 Committee and its successor under the Treaty of Amsterdam. From a UK perspective, these appear to be competing organisations based on completely opposed philosophies, doomed to failure. Yet are they actually mutually reconcilable steps on a road to effective supranational investigation? We are not the first group of political entities to travel this road. We should really look more closely at the USA version of the FBI before declaring a European cousin impossible.

The FBI does not operate alone. It is part of a network of federal-level organisations

like the Drugs Enforcement Agency (DEA), which deal with specific activities. It also operates alongside the other 40,000 local US law enforcement agencies, which also have horizontal cooperation procedures, as opposed to vertical cooperation procedures involving federal level agencies. Just as the European Union has no common Criminal Code, there is no Federal Common Law in the USA. The FBI has to operate under individual statutes passed by Congress of which there are over 200. These fall into three categories , according to a former Legal Attaché at the US Embassy :
• violations in which the USA itself is a victim;
• crime involving interstate or foreign commerce which needs to be investigated in conjunction with the FBI for reasons of logistics: interstate transportation of stolen property, aircraft hijacking, narcotics and the various organised crime and racketeering statutes;
• violations that can be more effectively investigated by a national organisation than a state one: - political corruption, terrorism, civil rights violation, espionage, political assassinations and other crimes with political overtones (Alderson & Tupman, 1989).

If the EU has the same law enforcement needs as the USA, it may be that the system that is developing can meet these needs without actually duplicating an FBI. It is easy to argue that the present situation is a chaotic alphabet soup, but a deeper examination of the arrangements already in place reveals that some order is emerging, although naturally problems remain.

Europe already has an institution that deals with law enforcement where the EU itself is a victim: UCLAF, dealing with fraud against the European Community Budget. This comes closest structurally to the FBI. It has a Director, who employs investigators who are not personnel seconded from the police services of other nation states. They serve one master and he serves the European Commission, a single master again. They do not have police powers, but seek to work through a single partner agency in each Member State. They possess a database so can coordinate intelligence and investigation, where the partner agency exists and is committed to assist, which is not the case in all countries.

Responding to the need for a set of procedures to allow non-federal cooperation between individual law enforcement bodies, there is the Schengen acquis, as we must now learn to call it, which provides a framework of operating procedures for day-to-day cross-border police cooperation. Now incorporated into the Treaty of Amsterdam, the UK and Ireland have opted out of its provisions, but are permitted to participate in individual aspects if they find them acceptable. Likewise, bizarrely, the non-Member States Norway and Iceland have opted in, despite not being members of the EU . This is because the Scandinavian states already had a mutual open border arrangement, as, of course do the UK and Ireland. Schengen establishes procedures for hot pursuit, requests for assistance in finding stolen property, witnesses and suspects.

The FBI exists to investigate interstate crimes where logistic support for such investigation is necessary. The problem for the EU is not one of logistics but one of incompatible justice systems. Stolen property that has crossed borders, and obtaining admissible witness statements from people in another state, are problems in the USA. Nevertheless, the legal systems of individual states are not based on different legal codes, with the possible exception of Louisiana, where some of the French legal system still exists. Schengen originally tried to bypass this problem through the medium of information technology. Communication was to be direct from VDU to VDU under the Schengen Information System. This devious attempt to bypass the legal system did not succeed. Schengen has had to settle for a halfway house, the SIRENE Bureaux. In these the many police agencies that coexist in single countries all sit in a single office, together with their supervising examining magistrates and procurators, depending on the particular criminal justice system. It is not just the British that have a genius for improvisation!

SIRENE 2 is on the way and presumably will be more streamlined. However comic opera the system may sound, it is a way of reconciling the French model of supervision of investigation by the examining magistrate with the system of supervision by the Procurator. Scotland could join it tomorrow, with very little difficulty. England and Wales, where supervision is by a superior police officer rather than a judicial officer, will take a little longer to reconcile. This is not a problem the FBI has to deal with in the USA, and is another reason why EU structures have taken another form. Nevertheless, Schengen provides good structures for cooperation between neighbouring police agencies separated by a politico-judicial border, when dealing with minor crimes.

Taking the third area of FBI responsibility, a supranational agency to investigate political crime is not something that individual Member States want or an area where agreement will be easy. There have been conflicting attitudes to particular causes pursued by individual terrorist groups. If immigration is substituted as the area of concern, then again Schengen has been a success in creating rules with regard to asylum, aliens, visas for third-country nationals, refugees and defining procedures for the EU's external borders. In this area there has been good cooperation with the K4 Committee set up by the Treaty of Maastricht to coordinate police cooperation policy throughout the European Union.

The area where European cooperation is not going well is that part of the second area of FBI competence identified above as coordinating responses to drug trafficking and organised crime. This programme, which involved the creation of Europol, was under the K4 Committee's auspices. Despite the production of a lengthy Convention, Europol has a long way to go before it gets anywhere near becoming an FBI. Article 2 of this Convention puts it in danger of being assigned too many areas of responsibility to achieve anything with the resources it has at present. It is also in danger of duplicating Interpol's very effective function as a message-exchange service. It should be restricted to a single crime, drug trafficking, and it should be given the personnel for it to carry out an intelligence gathering and analysis role on the lines of the Dutch CRI. Then its computer could be sensibly utilised. The attempt to get round legal problems by concentrating Europol resources into national bureaux in each Member State, and placing only a small group of liaison officers in the Netherlands, looks suspiciously like a duplication of the old Interpol system. The liaison officers look like a group of too few Indians, responsible to far too many chiefs.

An option that has not been properly explored for police services is the Customs model of the joint investigation team. The MAG '92 (Mutual Assistance Group) programme appears to have been able to anticipate and overcome the political and judicial difficulties of bringing together officers from different countries to investigate and prosecute the same case. Perhaps it is easier for European Treasuries to agree than European Home Offices and Ministries of Justice. Or perhaps Customs Officers do not operate under the same judicial supervision.

The time of a supranational European FBI has not yet come. But many aspects of a federal law-enforcement system are already in place. It now requires a major cause célèbre to complete the picture. Perhaps a major simultaneous terrorist atrocity in more than one capital city would do the trick. Certainly, media exposure of the trade in prostitutes, illegal immigrants, drugs, and counterfeit products has not produced an irresistible public demand for the next logical step to be taken. Equally, the public seems indifferent to FBI-style networked databases and the invasion of privacy inherent in them. As during Prohibition, organised criminal activity corrupts the whole system, and at the everyday level of evading duty on cigarettes and alcohol, rather than the high focus level of drug addiction.

The European Judicial Area

établir un droit pénal communautaire paraît l'unique solution viable face à la criminalité organisée. (Gil-Robles, 1997)

For some time fraud against the Community budget has been the main area in which the Commission has been able to take policy initiatives that affect all EU Home and Justice Affairs policy. The push via UCLAF towards the integration of Member States' investigative structures has had an impact in other areas, and the 1997/98 workplan moves another treasured project off the stocks. Section 5 rejoices in the title: 'Towards a European Judicial Area in the field of the Union's Financial Interests'. This takes matters forward, beyond article 209a. The Commission expects the European Parliament to ally with it against the Member States' governments, by pressing for a Community structure to ensure coordination, consultation and exchange of information on judicial cooperation against international financial crime. This is referred to, tantalisingly, as the Grotius project in the discussion at the European Parliament reported below. It further anticipates this will lead to a European prosecution liaison service (UCLAF, 1997/98). It commissioned the corpus juris study by a high level group of academics in response to a request by the parliament for a European Law Enforcement Area (UCLAF, 1996:1.1). Professor Delmas-Marty from the Sorbonne presented it to the European Parliament for discussion on 15 April 1997 (Senat).

According to Justice Carney, reported by the Irish Times, 9 June 1997, the corpus juris proposal is to establish a 'European Judicial Space', so that the territory of the EU would constitute a single legal area for the purposes of prosecuting fraud against the Community budget. A European Director of Public Prosecutions would have a head office in Brussels with offices in the capital cities of all Member States. Article 18 of the Corpus Juris proposals:

provides that for the purpose of the investigation, prosecution, trial and execution of sentence concerning the new created European budgetary crimes the territory of the Member States of the union shall constitute a single legal area.

The crimes will be market rigging, corruption or misuse of office by Community officials, misappropriation of funds, disclosure of secrets pertaining to office, money laundering and conspiracy. Crimes will be tried by a national independent court appointed by the Member State. Delmas-Marty proposed that the European Prosecutor General would be part of a Ministère Public Européen, which would also include a 'juge des libertés' to guarantee the rights of the defendant. These are far-reaching proposals, embodying different legal principles from those of England and Wales. No UK MEP is reported as joining the discussion.

Equally important, if IRENE 95 is to provide a true picture, is that all Member States notify UCLAF of frauds against the Community budget. A targeted strategy demands reliable, up-to-date information. A Commission proposal to improve both the level of detail and frequency of submission of Member States' reports of fraud and irregularities was to be adopted during 1996 (FAF, 1995:20).

According to Statewatch, a new IT project, called, unbelievably, GRASP, was initiated in February 1997, and is to be carried out by a consortium of EU police forces, businesses, universities and the Commission. This will attempt three novelties: it will be image-based, it will enable direct interrogation by one country of databases in another, and it will translate inquiries into the appropriate language when so doing (Statewatch, 1996). Statewatch is alarmed by the lack of EU-wide accountability of such projects, but there is a growing trend for the Commission to move into partnership with other organisations in the private and public sector. The Joint Research Centre of ISPRA is, for example, referred to in the UCLAF Work Programme as cooperating on risk analysis and improving the way relevant information is used (UCLAF, 1997/98:1.7). This must raise further questions about privacy as well as accountability and commercial secrecy.

Conclusion

Of necessity this book is impressionistic. It reflects conversations with and documentation assembled by helpful police trainers across the whole of the European Union. The authors have tried to make sense of their own experience and in the process may have omitted important variables because they did not encounter them as part of their learning process. There is room for many books in this field and for a great deal of further work. It is hoped that the information and arguments presented here will stimulate discussion and debate about the past, present and future of policing in Europe. It is too important for the whole system to be allowed to change by default. If it is to be done better, than at least let it be changed as a result of informed debate and not as a consequence of the implementation of a passing fashion in management doctrine.

Bibliography

ACPO, HMIC and Audit Commission, *Tackling Crime Effectively: Management Handbook*, London, HMSO, 1994.

Alderson, J.C., and Tupman, W. A. (eds) *Policing Europe after 1992* , Proceedings of an International Seminar, University of Exeter, 4-7 April 1989, Brookfield, Exeter, 1990.

AMSTERDAM, *Consolidated version of the Treaty on European Union*, Internet Address: http://europa.eu.int/abc/obj/amst/en/index.htm .

Amsterdam, *Questions and Answers, Q6, Q10, Q11,Q22*, Internet Address: http://europa.eu.int/abc/obj/amst/en/qa.htm .

Angell, I., Conference Paper delivered at Centre for Computer Security Research Conference, LSE, June 1996.

Brown, D., and Iles, S., 'Community Constables: A study of a police initiative' in Heal, K. (ed), *Police Today* , London, HMSO, 1985, pp. 43-59.

Cain, M., *Society and the Policeman's Role* , London, Routledge and Kegan Paul, 1973.

Carney, Justice, reported in *Irish Times* , 9.6.97.

Clarke, M., 'Citizenship, community and the management of crime' *British Journal of Sociology* , 27:4 (1987), pp. 384-393.

Critchley, T.A., *A History of Police in England and Wales 900-1966* , London, Constable, 1967.

De Figueiredo Dias, J. and Antunes, M. J., 'Portugal' in van den Wyngaert, C.(ed), *Criminal Procedure Systems in the European Community* , London, Butterworths, 1994, pp. 317-338.

EUROPA, 1995a, *Report of the Reflection Group*, June 2nd 1995, Part One, Section 1.B, para.45, Europa, the European Commission WorldWideWeb infobase document, Internet Address: http://www.cec.lu/en/agenda/igc-home/eu-doc/reflect/final_html#2.2 .

EUROPA, 1995b, 'The Netherland's position with respect to the 1996 IGC', *European Cooperation in the fields of Justice & Home Affairs, Third Memorandum for the 1996 Intergovernmental Conference*, Luxembourg, European Parliament, 8 December 1995. Europa, the European Commission WorldWideWeb infobase document, Internet Address: http://www.cec.lu/en/agenda/igc-home/ms-doc/state-nl/positn.html .

EUROPARL, *European Parliament's Briefings for the Intergovernmental Conference*, No. 1 'The Court of Justice'; No. 9 'Communitization of the Third Pillar [JHA] of the Treaty on European Union'; No. 26 'Europol'; No. 27 'The IGC and the Schengen Convention'; No. 28 'Combating Fraud against the Community Budget', Texts taken from Internet Address: http://www.europarl.eu.int/dg7/fiches/en/fiche1.htm .

FAF, *Protecting the Community's Financial Interests : The Fight Against Fraud Annual Report*, Brussels, European Commission, 1993,1994,1995,1996.

Gambetta, D., 'Inscrutable Markets', *Rationality and Society*, 6:3 (1994), pp. 353-68.

Gil-Robles, President of the European Parliament Public Hearing, Brussels, 15-26 April, 1997.

Goldstein, H., 'Police Discretion: the ideal versus the real', *Public Administration Review*, 23, 1963, pp. 140-48.

Goldstein, J., 'Police Discretion not to invoke the criminal process: low visibility decisions in the administration of justice', *Yale Law Journal* , 69, 1960, pp. 543-94.

Goodhart,A. L., 'Memorandum of Dissent', *Royal Commission on the Police 1962 Final Report*, London, HMSO, 1962, pp. 157-181.

Guardian ,10.6.96, p8.

Heal, K., and Morris, P., 'The effectiveness of patrol', in Heal, K. (ed), *Police Today*, London, HMSO, 1985.

Hough, M. and Mayhew, P., 'The British Crime Survey: First Report', *Home Office Research Study*, No 76, London, HMSO, 1983.

Interviews on non-attributable basis with police personnel in countries of the European Community 1988-1994.

Johnston, B., *Daily Telegraph* , 21.1.94.

Kelling, G. L., Pate, T., Dieckman, D., and Brown, C.E., *The Kansas City Preventive Patrol Experiment* , Washington DC., Police Foundation, 1974.

Kelling, G. L., 'On the Accomplishments of the Police', in Punch, M. (ed), *Control in Police Organisation,* Cambridge Massachusetts, MIT, 1983.

Maastricht, *The Unseen Treaty, Treaty on European Union,* Maastricht, David Pollard Publishing, Holmesdale Press, 1992.

Metropolitan Police, *Statement of Common Purpose and Values,* July 1997, Internet Address: http://www.open.gov.uk/police/mps/charter/socpv.htm .

Morgan, R., ' 'Policing by consent': legitimating the doctrine', in Morgan, R., and Smith, D.(eds), *Coming to Terms with Policing,* (1989), pp. 217-233.

Moylan, Sir J., *Scotland Yard and the Metropolitan Police,* London, Putnam and Co., 1934.

OJEC, 1995a, 'Notice No 95/C 316/01 : Council Act of 26 July 1995', drawing up the Convention based on Article K.3 of the Treaty on European Union, on the establishment of a European Police Office (Europol Convention), *Official Journal of the European Communities,* C 316 , Vol 38, 27th November, 1995, pp. 1-32.

OJEC, 1995b, 'Notice No 95/C 316/03 : Council Act of 26 July 1995', drawing up the Convention on the protection of the European Communities' financial interests, *Official Journal of the European Communities* , C 316, Vol 38, 27th November, 1995, pp. 48-57.

Politikan, reprinted in *Guardian* , 24.4.91.

Porter, J.H., 'Common Crime, law and policing in the English countryside 1600-1800', *Brookfield Papers,* No 2, Exeter, Brookfield, 1989.

Pougnet, N.G., 'Europol's IT systems - A Platform for Cutting-Edge Year 2000 Police Applications', *European Police and Government Security Technology,* January, 1998.

Poveda, T. G., *Lawlessness and Reform: the FBI in Transition,* Pacific Grove CA, Brooks/Cole, 1990.

Punch, M., and Naylor, T., 'The police: a social service', *New Society,* 17 May, 1973, pp. 358-361.

Reiner, R., *The Politics of the Police* , London, Harvester, 1985.

Reith, C., *A New Study of Police History*, Edinburgh and London, Oliver & Boyd, 1956.

Rennie, G. A., 'HM Customs and Excise IT and Intelligence Applications in Cross Border Control', *European Police Government and Security Technology* , January, 1998, pp. 8-9.

Rowan and Mayne, General Instructions, Part I. Discussed and quoted in Reith, C., *A New Study of Police History,* Edinburgh, Oliver & Boyd, 1956, pp. 135-6.

Royal Commission on the Police Final Report and Minutes of Evidence ,Cmnd 1728, London, HMSO, 1962.

Rumbaut, R.G., and Bittner, E., 'Changing Conceptions of the Police Role: A Sociological Perspective', *Crime and Justice,*1, 1979.

Scarman, Lord Justice, *The Scarman Report : The Brixton Disorders 10-12 April 1981,* reprinted London, Pelican, 1982.

Schmidhuber, 'Memorandum from Mr. Schmidhuber', *Protecting the Financial Interests of the Community: The Fight against Fraud, The Commission's Anti-Fraud Strategy Work Programme for 1994,* Brussels, European Commission, 21.3.94.

SEC, *SEC[95]249, Commission Communication* , Brussels, European Commission, 10.2.95.

Semerak, A.F. and Kratz, G., *Die Polizeien in Westeuropa,* Stuttgart, Boorberg, 1989.

Senat, *Senat Rapport* , no 352, Internet Address: http://www.senat.fr/rap/r96-352/r96-3527.html .

Shapland, J., and Vagg, J., 'Using the Police', *British Journal of Criminology,* 27:1 (1987), pp. 54-63.

Sigma, Autumn/Winter, 1996. Text from the World Wide Web edition.

Smith, G., *Politics of Western Europe,* Dartmouth, 5th edition, 1989, pp. 28-32.

Statewatch, Internet infobase, search performed on query Schengen from Internet homepage address: http://www.poptel.org.uk/statewatch/swhp.html/ .

Statewatch 1996, *Statewatch,* Vol 6, No 3, May-June 1996, reporting on article in *Police Science and Technology Review* , May 1996.

Trojanowicz, R., *An evaluation of the Neighbourhood Foot Patrol Program in Flint,* East Lansing, Michigan State University, 1982.

Tupman, W. A., 1992a, 'La démocratisation des services de police dans la nouvelle Communauté des États indépendants', *Les Cahiers de la sécurité intérieure,* 8: février-avril (1992), pp. 23-35.

Tupman, W. A., 1992b 'Ethics for Computer Technology and the Criminal Justice System', *Law, Computers and Artificial Intelligence,* 1:1 (1992), pp. 133-148.

Tupman, W. A., 1994a, 'Police Training Requirements in *The Face of New Types of Crime' The Challenges of the Third Millenium,* Vittoria, Basque Government Publications, pp. 37-62.

Tupman, W. A., 1994b, 'You should have read the small print:the European Commission's post-Maastricht response to Fraud', *Journal of Asset Protection and Financial Crime,* 2:2 (1994), pp. 107-114.

Tupman, W. A., 1994c, 'Can Cross-Border Policing be Other then Private Policing?', *Journal of Asset Protection and Financial Crime,* 1:4 (1994), pp. 286-287.

Tupman, W. A., 1995a, 'Cross-national Criminal Databases: the ongoing search for safeguards', *Journal of Law, Computers and Artificial Intelligence ,* 4: 3 (1995), pp. 261-275.

Tupman, W. A., 1995b, 'Keeping an eye on Eastern Europe', *Policing,* 11: 4 (1995), pp. 249-260.

Tupman, W. A., 1996, 'The Search for Supra-National Solutions: Investigating Fraud against the European Budget', *Hume Papers on Public Policy ,* 4: 3 (1996), pp. 43-54.

Tupman, W. A., 1997, revised version of above paper published in *Journal of Financial Crime ,* 1997, pp. 152-159.

Tupman, W. A., 1998a, 'Supranational Investigation after Amsterdam, the Corpus Juris and Agenda 2000', *Information and Communications Technology Law ,* 7: 2 (1998), pp. 85-102.

Tupman, W. A., 1998b, 'Violent Business? Networking, Terrorism and Organised Crime' in McKenzie, I.(ed), *Law, Power and Justice in England and Wales,* New York, Praeger, 1998.

Tupman, W. A., (forthcoming) 'Europe without Frontiers: Criminal Justice in Crisis', *Law, Computers and Artificial Intelligence.*

UCLAF, *The Fight Against Fraud Reports* listed under FAF above.

UCLAF, 1996, Internet information, 22.5.96. Homepage address: http//www.cwc.lu/en/eupol/fafr.html .

UCLAF WP, *Workplan for 97/8,* information on 20.3.98 at Internet homepage address: http:www.europa.eu.int/en/eupol/fafr.html .

UN, United Nations, *Fifth United Nations Survey of Crime Trends and Operations of Criminal Justice Systems 1990-1994 ,* Internet address: http//www.ifs.univie.ac.at/_uncjin/wcs.html .

van den Wyngaert, C. (ed), *Criminal Procedure Systems in the European Community,* London, Butterworths, 1994.

van Duyne, P., 'Organised crime markets in a turbulent Europe', *European Journal on Criminal Policy and Research ,* 1:3, pp. 10-30.

Weatheritt, M., 'Community Policing: how does it work and how we know, a review of research', in Bennett, T.(ed), *The Future of Policing ,* Cambridge, Cropwood Conference Papers, 1983, pp. 127-145.

Wilson, J.Q., and Boland, B., 'The Effect of the Police on Crime', *Law and Society Review ,* 12 (1977-1978), pp. 367-390.